CHEERS MY ARSE!

Also by Ricky Tomlinson

Ricky
Football My Arse!
Celebrities My Arse!
Reading My Arse!

CHEERS MY ARSE!

Ricky Tomlinson

sphere

SPHERE

First published in Great Britain in 2007 by Sphere

A CIP catalogue record for this book is available
from the British Library

ISBN 978-1-84744-168-3

Typeset in Melior and Akzidenz Grotesk by M Rules
Printed and bound in Great Britain by
Clays Ltd, St Ives plc
Paper supplied by Hellefoss AS, Norway

Sphere
An imprint of
Little, Brown Book Group
100 Victoria Embankment
London EC4Y 0DY

An Hachette Livre UK Company

www.littlebrown.co.uk

To Rita and Jackie. Cheers!

Acknowledgements

I am raising a glass in a toast of thanks to the entire Sphere/ Little, Brown team, and in particular Antonia Hodgson, for their expert help in getting published this fourth book in the *My Arse* series. I am indebted to Ian Allen and Michael Giller for their safety-net checking work on the hundreds of anecdotes that have been knitted together to make *Cheers My Arse!* the most complete compilation of funny booze stories ever! I gratefully acknowledge the following websites as being first-class points of reference:

- www.anecdotage.com
- www.IMBd.com
- www.en.wikipedia.org
- www.celebritywonder.com
- www.brainyquote.com.

Thanks to Peter Cotton for a perfectly tailored jacket, to Tamsyn Berryman and Philip Parr for their editorial support, and to Kezia Storr at PA Photos and Linda Silverman for help on picture research. Most of all, thanks to all my pals in and around the worlds of television, showbusiness, films and sport who have so willingly helped me dig out the stories. You are too many to mention, but you know who you are! A lot of the tales have been recalled through hazy memories of drunken nights (and sometimes days), so I cannot guarantee their total authenticity. Finally, thanks to my good pal Norman Giller for his diligent guidance, and to Rita for being there. And Norman thanks Jackie Jones for helping him find the right rhythm.

This one's on me. Cheers my arse!

Contents

Opening Time by Ricky Tomlinson

Pull up a stool and join me here at the bar . . . just for a laugh. The purpose of this book is to keep you amused, a little bemused and just occasionally confused. In fact, it will have all the effects of a good drink, except for the hangover.

I am a strictly mild and bitter man myself, but I have hilarious stories to share with you that cover the entire range of the boozing business – from the public bar through to the champagne socialists and the sozzled aristocracy.

There are tales of the unexpected about pie-eyed politicians, smashed sportsmen, intoxicated television and film stars, off-their-head rock musicians, rat-arsed Rat Pack members and all sorts of people perfectly happy in their pursuit of being piss artists.

It is important, I feel, not to glamorise drinking. It can be harmful to the health, as I know only too well from harrowing experiences with loved ones and close friends. There's a lot of sense in the old Chinese proverb: 'First the man takes a drink, then the drink takes a drink, then the drink takes the man.'

But there is no escaping the fact that the best times are often had when drinks are flowing, and – let's be honest – there is nothing as funny as the drunk trying to pretend to be sober and insisting: 'I'm not so think as you drunk I am.'

A while back I was on a book-promotion tour in Ireland and

we stopped at a small country pub on our way into Dublin. The little wizened landlord came out, threw his arms open in despair and said: 'I'm so sorry fellas, but we don't open for another thirty minutes.' He paused for a moment, then added: 'Now would you be liking a drink while you're waiting?'

The landlord had no idea why we found it so funny, and it triggered a thought in my head that this would make a great subject for the next book in the *My Arse* series.

So, together with my writing partner Norman Giller, we started to gather the best drinking stories, leaning heavily on our many mates in the worlds of showbusiness, television, the theatre and sport to feed us with their best booze-related stories.

Here's one I got from my fellow Scouser, comedian Stan 'The Jeermans' Boardman:

A distressed man, in his eighties, is crying in a Liverpool pub, struggling to finish his pint. The barman approaches him and asks what's wrong.

The old man replies: 'I just got married to a beautiful twenty-five-year-old woman. She was everything I ever dreamed of.'

'Don't worry, pal,' the barman says sympathetically. 'It may seem that you don't have a lot in common, but maybe this is an opportunity for each of you to work out your differences.'

The old man shakes his head. 'No, there are no differences,' he says. 'We have loads in common, and agree on everything! She's smart, funny, and wonderful to be around.'

The barman looks at the man, confused. 'So you're worried she just married you for your money, then?' he asks.

'No, it's definitely not that,' the old man says. 'She's an heiress and completely independent. She's ten times wealthier than I'll ever be.'

The barman suddenly nods in understanding. 'It's a sex problem, isn't it?' he says. 'I can help you out there. I've got some Viagra tablets.'

The old man just shakes his head and howls, 'No, no. She's great in bed and I have no problems in that department. We make love morning, noon and night.'

The barman gives him a look of total bewilderment. 'It sounds like you've got the perfect relationship,' he says. 'So why the hell are you so upset and crying?'

The old man wails: 'I can't remember where I live!'

Now that, of course, is a joke. But most of the stories you are about to read are perfectly true, and they usually involve famous people. I have occasionally changed the names to protect the guilty, and I've made it clear when I think the stories that have been handed on to me are possibly exaggerated or apocryphal.

The only criteria for them getting into my book was that they had to be funny.

Here they are for your pleasure and amusement. Drink up and enjoy.

Cheers My Arse!

Ricky Tomlinson

Bar-room Tales of the Unexpected

Many moons ago, when I was first starting out at the acting lark, there was an old thespian who used to love to imbibe, and as he strode into a pub he would open his arms and theatrically quote the eighteenth-century poet William Shenstone:

Whoe'er has travelled life's dull round,
Where'er his stages may have been,
May sigh to think he still has found
The warmest welcome at an inn.

That bloke Shenstone knew what he was talking about, and here in the new millennium the sentiments of his words are equally true. You can't beat the atmosphere and camaraderie of a pub.

Some of my happiest times have been in Liverpool pubs, sharing stories and jokes with my mates (often while the leg of lamb was over-roasting at home). We used to have secretive and impromptu lock-ins, with pub landlords allowing carefully selected customers to stay behind drinking after hours. This, of course, was in an era when pubs had strict licensing laws, and we used to dread the 'Time, gentlemen, please' shouts at eleven o'clock.

One Londonderry publican didn't quite grasp the idea of

I'm on my way to a bring-your-own booze party, with my pal Les Bather. Cheers my arse!

restricting lock-ins to a trusted handful of customers. He lost his licence when a police raid revealed one hundred and forty people supping after hours in his pub.

I used to be able to direct people around Liverpool by the geographical positions of the pubs before the bulldozers moved in and changed the face of the city for ever. There were places like the Garrick, the Halfway House, the Honky Tonk, the Toxteth, the Crown, the Vines, Lulu's, the Britannia, the Mediterranean, the Bow and Arrow, the Cumberland Arms and the Thirlmere, where we used to drink shoulder to shoulder with Everton footballers in the era when they were being paid just a few bob more than the average earner. Back in those days of my drinking youth a pub crawl quickly became a stagger.

Liverpool was without argument the drinking capital of Britain, if not the world. Early in the twentieth century they reckon that one in every seven buildings in the city was selling booze, and there were 24,342 licences issued in one year alone on Merseyside. Loads of people were turning their parlours into one-room 'snug' pubs. In those days you never walked (or reeled) alone in Liverpool.

I've supped in many of the boozers, and can't remember having anything but good times and loads of laughs in each of them. I particularly recall a character from the old Mediterranean pub called Joe Murray, who had a screamingly obvious syrup (syrup of figs – wig) and used to drive around in a big flash American car. He was a bit of a Robin Hood who was into some uh, enterprising business deals, but used to give away wads of cash to old-age pensioners and people on their uppers. None of the grateful recipients ever asked where the money came from.

The police kept a close eye on Joe in the hope that they could find an excuse to take him down to the station for questioning, and one day a copper thought he'd got him when he staggered out of the Mediterranean with a mate and they both clambered unsteadily into the American motor. This was pre-breathalyser days.

The officer, sitting in his patrol car, waited for Joe to drive a few hundred yards and then pulled him over. He sauntered to the side of Joe's car and signalled for him to wind down the window.

'Been drinking, Mr Murray?' the officer asked, knowing full well that Joe was next to legless.

'Shertainly have, Offisher,' slurred Joe. 'I'm as drunk as a shkunk.'

'In that case,' said Officer Plod, 'I want you to get out of the car and accompany me to the police station, where you will be charged with driving while under the influence of alcohol.'

Joe's mate leaned across and said: 'Excuse me, Officer, but I'm stone-cold sober and am fit to drive. This is an American car and Joe is in the passenger seat.'

The Britannia pub in Stanley Road was run by a veteran publican called Tom McCain, who could brag for Britain. He'd been there, done that and always had a story to top any that his customers came up with.

You couldn't take offence at old Tom because he told his stories with such passion and conviction that it seemed only polite to let him think you believed every word. But some of his tales were taller than the Liver Buildings. According to him, he killed more Japs during the war than John Wayne and took the D-Day beaches on his own.

Tom owned a magnificent Staffordshire bull terrier called Butch, and he claimed it was the most intelligent dog not only in Liverpool but in the entire world.

One day – and my brother Albert swears he was a witness to this – a crowd of Norwegian sailors were making a fuss of the dog, so Tom got Butch to perform a series of tricks. It built up towards a climax in which, to shouted instructions from Tom, Butch leapt up on to the bar and came down with a bag of crisps between his teeth.

'Open them,' ordered Tom, and Butch ripped open the bag of crisps.

'Salt!' called Tom, and Butch nosed the crisps out of the way until he found the little blue sachet of salt and nudged it to Tom's feet.

The Norwegian sailors applauded.

Then, as Tom pointed, Butch went out into the yard and came back in with half a brick clasped in his mouth.

Tom patted him on the head and Butch swaggered off down the cellar stairs.

'What's he going to do with the brick?' one of the sailors asked.

'He's going to build himself a new kennel,' said Tom, with a poker face.

And I think the sailors really believed him.

That, I hope, has set the mood for my bar-room tales of the unexpected . . .

The licensing laws when I was a young drinker were a pain in the arse. Of course, now they have gone to the other daft extreme where many pubs are open twenty-four hours a day. Me and my mates would have drunk the Mersey dry if that had been the case at our boozing peak. You lack discipline when you're young, and I should know, because I lost my way a few times.

To get round the stupid opening-and-closing laws of my drinking days crafty Scousers opened all types of drinking and social clubs so that still-thirsty people had places to go to when the pubs shut. Many of the clubs got round the laws by serving food while customers supped. Other, more shady places somehow knew if and when police raids were planned. Now I wonder where they got their info? Let's just say that many's the time I've stood alongside coppers in and out of uniform supping at barely legal bars.

One of the most infamous clubs was the Colombo, which some old-timers might remember as the Rum Runner or Maggie May's. Those were the days when I was known as Hobo Rick, touring the pubs and clubs with our group, the Hi-Fi Three. As well as singing skiffle and standards, we used to put on comedy shows for punters who were three parts pissed.

The Colombo was notorious for being the haunt of some of Liverpool's hardest criminals, professional gangsters who packed guns and could have stepped out of the *Godfather* films, apart from the fact they talked in thick Scouse: 'I'll make you an offer you can't refuse . . . pal.'

One night while we were performing at the Colombo somebody fired both barrels of a shotgun. We all dived for cover, and I finished up hiding underneath one of those leather pub floormats. A fat lot of good that would have done me if the shots had come my way.

Suddenly the club's owner, Tony Gallagher, a little guy who had been a bantamweight boxer, hopped over the bar, jumped on stage and grabbed our microphone.

'This is the last straw,' he announced. 'I'm not going to stand for this sort of thing in my club any more. From now on, nobody, and I mean *nobody*, is allowed in without a tie.'

It was the Scouse equivalent of Basil Fawlty saying, 'No riff-raff.'

I once had a barmaid tell me, in all seriousness, that she listened to more confessions than any Catholic priest. When you analyse it, she was probably telling the truth, because many people see the pub as a sort of sanctuary, an escape from the stresses and strains of life. When their tongues have been loosened by alcohol, people feel they can unburden themselves to the barmaid or the landlord without being judged and given two hundred Hail Marys.

One customer at a Midlands pub got the landlord's wife feeling very sorry for him; so sorry that when he revealed he was not getting any nookie at home, she volunteered to . . . let him have some on account.

She took him into a room at the back of the pub and let him have his way. What she forgot was that, because of a series of burglaries, her husband had installed CCTV security cameras in every room.

Imagine the husband's reaction when he was idly watching the bank of security screens to see his wife giving a customer more than a pint of Guinness. He got a baseball bat that he always kept behind the bar and went to the room where the act was taking place. The customer was still in the throes of passion when the door swung open, but he performed the quickest *coitus interruptus* in history, getting a whack across the bum as he made his exit with his trousers around his ankles.

The landlord was later divorced by his wife on the grounds of unreasonable behaviour.

The customer had bruised buttocks but a great anecdote to tell his mates. Cheers My Arse!

One of the best barmaid stories I've heard came from a Scouse pal of mine who lived in New York for a couple of years. She was a buxom girl who worked in a bar in Manhattan, and she gave as good as she got from the leering customers who turned everything into innuendo.

One night a drunk was giving her a really hard time, and she got so fed up with his vile tongue and crude propositions that she slipped a sleeping draught into his drink. Then, with him asleep with his head on his arms, she superglued his tie to the bar.

When he woke up hours later he nearly broke his neck trying to leave the bar.

Superglue was also used to startling effect in a Tokyo pole-dancing bar, this time by a disgruntled punter who had been snubbed by one of the girls. He put glue on her pole just before she started her dance, and they had to cut her G-string off to release her.

Police arrested the punter and stuck him in prison.

A new phenomenon since my regular supping days is the introduction of pub bouncers. We used to sort out problems ourselves, and there were plenty of publicans on Merseyside who were capable of giving any troublemakers a slap, if necessary.

Mind you, I realised the need for bouncers when I read about the drunk in Leicester who was banned from every pub in the land. After being thrown out of the Galaxy in Burbage he returned and terrified everybody with a revving chainsaw. I would have said to the landlord, 'For Gawd's sake, let him have some peanuts with his pint.'

I had mixed feelings when I heard about Lisa Jones – a strapping, six-foot father of two – being banned from the Jacob's Well pub in the village of Honley, near Huddersfield, because she kept using the ladies' toilet. The forty-three-year-old transsexual launched a sex-discrimination claim and won her case and a thousand quid compensation. All I wanted to know was whether she left the toilet seat up or down?

Getting banned from the boozer reminds me of one of the oldest Shakespeare jokes. Will the Quill walked into his local inn at Stratford-on-Avon and stood pondering at the bar, saying aloud: 'To beer, or not to beer.' The landlord was not amused and said: 'Get out . . . you're bard.'

It was reported in the Belfast *Telegraph* back in the 1970s that an Alcoholics Anonymous meeting had ended in a drunken brawl after more than three hundred pounds had been spent at the bar where they were meeting as a challenge to prove they could sit in a pub without drinking.

Police called in to break up the fighting did not press charges and declined to give any names to the reporter. 'They wish to remain anonymous,' a police spokesman said.

The Luxembourg branch of Alcoholics Anonymous was much more peaceful when first formed, but then it had only two members.

There would be a lot of contenders for the title 'Rudest Pub Landlord' but Norman Balon has to be the favourite. He was so offensive that he made Al 'Pub Landlord' Murray seem positively friendly and welcoming.

He ran the Coach and Horses in Greek Street, Soho, for more than fifty years and became so infamous for his wicked tongue that he was immortalised with a regular feature in *Private Eye*. He was also the menacing off-stage presence in Keith Waterhouse's hilarious play *Jeffrey Bernard Is Unwell*, which features the late *Spectator* columnist locked in the bar of the Coach and Horses, which for him was the

Peter O'Toole, portraying Jeffrey Bernard, outside the famous Soho watering hole The Coach and Horses. It was run by the rudest landlord in the west.

equivalent of being trapped in paradise. Peter O'Toole and Tom Conti have both played the title role on stage. For O'Toole it was almost typecasting, but Conti – famously a teetotaller – had to reach really far into his acting boots.

Balon's stock opening line to a customer arriving in his pub would be: 'What the f****** hell do you want?'

He could hardly complete a sentence without the f-word, and would deliberately ignore customers waiting to be served until they were almost reduced to begging for a drink.

'I can't get any f****** peace and quiet around here,' he'd say. 'Why don't you f*** off to a pub where you'd be welcome?'

If he didn't like the look of someone, he would say straight to their faces: 'You're barred, you bastard.' He used that as the title of his autobiography, which has become such a collectors' item that first editions now fetch £250 on the internet.

My favourite Norman Balon story goes back to the days when he was *genuinely* rude and angry, rather than just trying to live up to his reputation by insulting customers who visited the Coach and Horses in the hope of receiving an ear-bashing from the master.

A jazz musician, carrying his alto saxophone in a case, came in for a drink on his way to a gig in Soho. He innocently put his case on the bar, and asked Balon for a large Scotch.

The landlord eyed the musician and then the saxophone case. 'Get that f****** thing off of my bar,' he snapped.

'It's my saxophone,' said the customer.

'I don't give a f*** if it's a telephone,' said Balon, 'get it off my bar.'

The saxophonist was slow to remove it, so nutty Norm grabbed hold of the case and hurled it across the bar towards the door.

'Now f*** off with your phone,' he shouted to the stunned jazzman. 'You're barred, you bastard.'

They don't make them like Norman Balon any more . . . thank f***!

The thirstiest customers were those of the Fox and Goose pub in Birmingham, which did not have any beer delivered between August 1975 and October 1977 because of a dispute with draymen.

Once peace had been restored, there was a huge celebration organised for the reopening of the pub on 31 October 1977.

There were loud cheers as the landlord prepared to pull the first pint, which quickly gave way to jeers when the glass remained empty. There had been a power cut which put all the pumps out of action. The long dry spell continued.

I'm not sure I believe the following story, but it was passed on to me as being authentic. I think I should issue a warning that if you are of a nervous disposition, you may want to give it a miss.

A friend of a friend, let's call him Phil, went to the Far East for an important business meeting. Afterwards, he had time to kill before his flight back to Heathrow, so he went to a local bar for a drink.

He'd just finished his first drink when a very attractive Oriental woman approached and asked if she could buy him another. He was surprised but flattered. 'How could I refuse?' he said with a smile, turning on the charm.

The woman walked to the bar and brought back two more drinks – one for her and one for him. Phil thanked her, clinked his glass against hers and then took a sip. And that was the last thing he remembered . . . until he woke up not knowing what day it was. He discovered he was lying in a hotel bathtub, his body submerged in ice.

Phil looked around frantically, trying to figure out where he was and how he had got there. Then he spotted the note: DON'T MOVE. CALL THE HOTEL OPERATOR.

A telephone rested on the side of the bathtub. Phil picked up the receiver and dialled zero, his fingers numb from the ice. He explained to the operator that he was in a bath of ice and in desperate need of assistance.

The operator seemed oddly familiar with his predicament. She said calmly and firmly, 'Sir, I want you to reach behind you, slowly and carefully. Is there a tube protruding from your lower back?'

Nervously, Phil felt around behind him. Sure enough, there was a tube.

The operator said, 'Sir, don't panic, but one of your kidneys has been harvested. There's a ring of organ thieves operating in this city, and it seems they have got to you. I will get a doctor and paramedics to you straight away. Don't move until they arrive.'

The moral is: don't accept drinks from strange women; otherwise it could be harvest time for you, too. I've heard of drinks costing an arm and a leg, but this is ridiculous.

At the last count, there were more than sixty thousand pubs in the United Kingdom, and as long ago as 1393 King Richard II ordered landlords to erect signs with pictures portraying the name of their premises. Many people in the Middle Ages were illiterate and they were able to use the pictures as signposts as well as discovering where they could get their ale.

When you see a pub sign featuring the word 'Three' it is usually based on the arms of the London livery companies (or trade guilds, which I know all about, having passed my City and Guilds as a master plasterer): *Three Arrows* (The Worshipful Company of Fletchers), *Three Bucks* (The Leathersellers), *Three Castles* (The Masons), *Three Compasses* (The Carpenters), *Three Crowns* (The Drapers), *Three Cups* (The Salters), *Three Goats' Heads* (The Cordwainers), *Three Hammers* (The Blacksmiths), *Three Horseshoes* (The Farriers), *Three Tuns* (The Brewers and the Vintners), *Three Wheatsheafs* (The Bakers).

I've always been fascinated by the names and histories of our pubs, such as the Eagle, mentioned in the 'Pop Goes the Weasel' nursery rhyme: 'Up and down the City Road/In and out the Eagle/That's the way the money goes/Pop goes the weasel.' After some homework, I've discovered that the 'weasel' is Cockney rhyming slang for a coat (weasel and stoat), and 'popping the weasel' means that after a bevy at the Eagle, which is in Islington, the customer pawns his coat to help pay for the next drinking session.

But my favourite pub name is the Nowhere Inn in Plymouth. If you're late home from there and your missus says, 'Where have you been?' you can truthfully say, 'Nowhere.'

I'm allowing my writing partner Norman Giller in here with a true story that shows all's not always fair in love and drinking. His dad, George, was an East End pub pianist at the Crooked Billet in the notorious Cable Street, where Norm was born in the same year as me (Hitler heard the news of the two of us arriving and ordered the Blitz).

George, who doubled as a bookie's runner in the days before betting shops, used to get paid thirty bob (£1.50) for his weekend piano-playing, but he would sup so much beer that at settling-up time on the Monday he owed the publican money. And thirty bob's worth of beer in those days was enough to launch a battleship. We are talking a shilling (5p) a pint!

Now, in spite of all evidence to the contrary, Norm fancies himself as a bit of a joanna player, too, so one day during a drinking session at the Crooked Billet he filled in at the piano while his dad went for a leak. As he started tinkling away at the ivories in his banana-fingered way, a drunken docker who was as wide as he was tall staggered over to the piano.

'Play "I'll Take You Home Again, Kathleen",' he slurred.

'I can't,' said Norm, having nearly exhausted his repertoire of a couple of jazz tunes.

'You're f****** useless,' said the docker.

Cockily and stupidly, Norm stood up and said: 'Well, you play it better.'

An alcohol-fuelled red mist came down on the docker, who grabbed featherweight Norman in a bear hug and gave him the old Cockney kiss with his forehead. His equally drunk mates joined in, and when Norm's father came out of the gents' he was greeted with the sight of his son disappearing under a welter of bodies.

A pro-class boxer in his army days, George piled in and started thumping the enemy, without a clue as to what had started it all.

The publican, a six-foot-six giant called Les, leapt over the top of the bar, took rapid stock of the situation, decided he couldn't handle the half-dozen dockers, and went for the easy option. So George and Norm were duly tossed out on to the street.

He had thrown his own pianist out of the pub!

Norm had only been in there to celebrate landing his first job in Fleet Street, so the following Monday he reported to the *Evening Standard* sports desk with a belter of a black eye.

A regular drinker at Thirsty Kirsty's, a pub in Dunfermline, was banned by the landlord in the spring of 2007 for incessant farting. Sounds like a trumped-up charge to me.

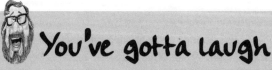

You've gotta laugh

A down-at-heel bloke goes into a Liverpool bar and orders a drink. The barman says, 'No way, pal. I don't think you can pay for it.'

'You're right,' the man confesses. 'I don't have any money, but if I show you something you haven't seen before, will you give me a drink?'

'You have a deal, pal,' says the barman.

The man reaches into his coat pocket and pulls out a mouse. He puts the mouse on the bar and it runs down the side, across the room, up the piano, on to the keyboard and starts playing Chopin's 'Minute Waltz'. He plays it so well that he finishes it in thirty seconds.

The barman applauds, and admits, 'You're right . . . I've never seen anything like that before. That mouse is really gifted.'

The man downs his drink and asks the barman for another.

'Will that be cash or another miracle, pal?' asks the barman.

'Watch this,' replies the man. Again, he reaches into his coat, but this time he pulls out a frog. He puts the frog on to the bar, and it starts to sing.

The frog has a marvellous voice and perfect pitch. A stranger from the other end of the bar hurries over to the man and offers him three hundred pounds for the frog.

'It's a deal,' says the man, taking the money and handing over the frog. The stranger runs out of the bar before he can change his mind.

'Are you some kind of nut?' asks the barman. 'You sold a singing frog for three hundred quid? It could have been worth millions. You must be crazy.'

'Not me,' says the man. 'The mouse is a ventriloquist.'

Hark Who's Talking About Drink

'He was a wise man who invented beer.'
- Plato

'He was an even wiser man who drank the beer.'
- Ken Dodd

'The problem with the world is that everyone is a few drinks behind.'
- Humphrey Bogart

'Always do sober what you said you'd do drunk. That will teach you to keep your mouth shut.'
- Ernest Hemingway

'Just remember that I have taken more out of alcohol than alcohol has taken out of me.'
- Winston Churchill

'Sir, if you were my husband, I would poison your drink.'
- Lady Astor to Winston Churchill

'Madam, if you were my wife, I'd drink it.'
- Churchill's reply

'Time is never wasted when you're wasted all the time.'
- Jeffrey Bernard

'Work is the curse of the drinking class.'
- Oscar Wilde

'When I read about the evils of drinking, I gave up reading.'
- Henny Youngman

'Beer is proof that God loves us and wants us to be happy.'
- Benjamin Franklin

'I think, therefore I drink.'
- Dickie Henderson

'Wine is bottled poetry.'
- Robert Louis Stevenson

'He who drinks last drinks longest.'
- John Edwards

'Drink turns fools into brave men and brave men into fools.'
- Peter Sellers

'I think a man ought to get drunk at least twice a year just on principle, so he won't let himself get snotty about it.'
- Raymond Chandler

'Give me a woman who truly loves beer and I will conquer the world.'
- Kaiser Wilhelm

'He who makes a beast of himself through drink at least rids himself of the pain of being a man.'
– Samuel Johnson

'I would kill everyone in this room for a drop of sweet beer.'
– Homer Simpson

'They who drink beer will think beer.'
– Washington Irving

'You're not drunk if you can lie on the floor without holding on.'
– Dean Martin

2 Order! Order!

Drink does not discriminate. Rich man, poor man, beggarman, thief – it can make bloody fools of all of us. Lords, presidents, kings and queens, and the working class that I'm proud to come from have all been made to look silly arses by alcohol.

I'm from a generation used to having hard drinkers in charge of the country. Winston Churchill was about to become Prime Minister when I was born, and few leaders could put away the booze like Winnie. His family have fought hard to protect his image and insist that most of the Scotch he consumed was so watered down that it was no more potent than mouthwash. Well, I reckon that's a load of hogwash. As far back as 1924 he wrote to his 'darling Clementine': 'I drink champagne at all meals and buckets of claret and whisky and soda in between.'

It has been well documented that he liked to take his first whisky and soda soon after breakfast and that for the rest of the day the tumbler was rarely empty. After his regular afternoon nap he would have two or three glasses of iced whisky and soda before dinner, at which he always had champagne, then several shots of brandy. Before bed it would be back to the whisky and soda routine.

When you think he was consuming all this while running (and winning) a war, it is an eye-opener.

In April 1940, with Hitler preparing for the Blitz on London,

Winston had difficulty completing a speech in the House of Commons and had to be led away from the Dispatch Box. Cecil King, the powerhouse behind the *Daily Mirror*, was a witness and wrote: 'It is at times like these that age and excessive brandy drinking tell.'

In the same year an envoy for US President Franklin D. Roosevelt reported: 'It was quite obvious that he had consumed a good many whiskies before I arrived. But during a monologue on how Britain would win the war he became quite sober.'

Roosevelt later observed: 'Churchill is the best man England has, even if he is drunk half the time.' It's doubtful that the President cared too much – after all, he had had the good sense to repeal the Prohibition Act a few years earlier.

Churchill's Cabinet colleagues used to go to great lengths to avoid getting trapped in late-night drinking sessions with him. Rab Butler confessed that when 'the old man' wasn't looking he would pour his brandy into his shoe because he simply could not keep pace with the PM. A weird case of having your drinks laced!

This all brings me to a memorable exchange that Churchill – so legend has it – had with my larger-than-life local MP Bessie Braddock.

Bessie, God bless her, looked like the back of a bus, but she had a heart the size of Anfield and was a fiery and totally committed socialist, serving as an outspoken Liverpool MP for twenty-four years. She and Churchill were poles apart in outlook, background and political persuasion.

Seeing the PM in an obviously less than sober state, Bessie said: 'Winston, you're drunk.'

'Bessie,' he said, 'you are ugly . . . but in the morning I'll be sober.'

Churchill was the wittiest but by no means the heaviest drinker in the House, where perhaps it would be more appropriate if the Speaker shouted: 'Orders! Orders!'

George Brown (no relation to Gordon) takes the title for the most spectacular drunk in the post-war House of Commons.

For those too young to remember, he was Foreign Secretary and Deputy Leader of the Labour Party during Harold Wilson's reign. He was a Lambeth-born Cockney with a high intellect but a low resistance to booze.

When Wilson and Brown were pitched against each other in a head-to-head duel for the leadership of the party, their Labour colleague Anthony Crosland had no fear of being prosecuted for slander when he described the contest as 'a choice between a crook [Wilson] and a drunk [Brown]'.

It had long been rumoured that Brown had a drink problem, and it became the currency of public debate following the assassination of President John F. Kennedy in 1963.

Brown was invited by ITV to pay tribute to Kennedy on the night of the murder because he had been closely associated with the President. He went to the studio direct from a dinner where he had drunk himself the wrong side of sobriety, and he was then plied with more drink in the green room before the programme.

Also in the green room was the actor Eli Wallach, who was there to give an American slant on the assassination. Brown was so belligerent towards him that studio staff had to pull them apart as they squared up to each other.

When Brown was finally positioned in front of the cameras it was obvious that he was out of his head, and he interpreted a perfectly fair question as implying he had exaggerated his closeness to the President. What should have been a tribute to JFK became a rambling, slurred and incoherent attack on the show's host. Later, Brown had to issue a public apology for his behaviour. He put it down to the fact that he was grief-stricken by the President's death, but there were many more drunken gaffes to follow.

It got to the point where the satirical magazine *Private Eye* had to find a new way of saying 'drunk' – the adjective that best described Brown on numerous occasions but could have led to libel action. They settled on a euphemism that has become part of our language – 'tired and emotional'.

In 1967 Brown, in his role as Foreign Secretary, negotiated for

Britain to join the European Economic Community, but he had his feet taken from under him by a curt and dismissive '*non*' from French President Charles de Gaulle.

From then on, his conduct became increasingly erratic. It is part of political folklore that he embarrassed himself while drunk at an official reception in South America. He was reported to have swayed over to a tall, elegant vision in red, and requested the honour of 'dancing this waltz', only to be informed: 'I will not dance with you for three reasons. The first is that you are drunk. The second is that the band is not playing a waltz, but the Peruvian national anthem. The final reason is that I am the Cardinal Archbishop of Montevideo.'

There was a final humiliation for George in the 1970s when he was photographed falling down in the street at Westminster and crawling along the gutter, obviously the worse for wear.

He was put out to grass and became Lord George-Brown, consumed by a hatred of Harold Wilson (who always made sure he was photographed holding a working man's pint, while it was well known in private that he hit the brandy bottle).

It was *The Times* that printed a widely held opinion that 'Lord George-Brown drunk is a better man than Prime Minister Harold Wilson sober.'

It would have been a good contest between George Brown and maverick Tory MP Alan Clark as to which of them could sink the most liquor. To date, Clark is the only Member of Parliament to have been accused in the Commons of being drunk at the Dispatch Box. In 1983, while Minister of Employment, he was making a reading of a bill after a wine-tasting dinner. The complexities of the legislation were suddenly too complicated for him to explain properly, and Labour MP Clare Short stood up and made the accusation.

Clark listed his considerable drinking exploits in his 1993 book *The Alan Clark Diaries* (Weidenfeld & Nicolson), and wrote of the unique challenge of being drunk and trying to disguise it:

Suddenly I was aware of a voice shouting, 'Point of Order, Mr Deputy Speaker.' I sat down, knowing that I had in my drunken stupor missed several pages from my speech. A new Labour member, whom I had never seen before, called Clare Short, dark-haired and serious with a lovely Brummie accent, said something about she'd read that you couldn't accuse a fellow member of being drunk, but she really believed I was incapable. 'It is disrespectful,' she went on, 'to the House and to the office that he holds that he should come here in this condition.' She was right, of course. I was incapable and very, very drunk.

What a life he led. He was once cited in a divorce case in South Africa in which it was revealed he'd had affairs with Valerie Harkess, the wife of a South African judge, and *both* of her daughters, Josephine and Alison. After sensationalist tabloid headlines, Clark's wife Jane remarked upon what Clark had called 'the coven' with the crushing line: 'Well, what do you expect when you sleep with below stairs types?' She referred to her husband as an 'S, H, One, T'.

A light went out on the Westminster stage when Clark died at the age of seventy-one in 1999.

More recently, of course, former Lib-Dem leader Charles Kennedy has admitted that he is an alcoholic. Who will ever forget his last major speech at Southport as leader of his party when the television cameras showed him perspiring profusely and with tell-tale shaking hands. Onlookers had visions of him going home in a bucket as the sweat cascaded off him.

I admired him for his honesty in later standing up and confessing that he had a major problem, and I'm convinced he's still got a lot to give to politics, provided he can beat the demon drink.

It seems that Liberal leaders are often a bit too liberal! Jeremy Thorpe

Charles Kennedy caught out drinking again, but this is the cup that cheers.

was 'outed' back in the days when being gay was considered unacceptable, and then he topped that by being accused of hiring an assassin to bump off a former male lover he claimed was trying to blackmail him.

Paddy Ashdown got exposed in a straight affair, and was condemned by the tabloid headline: 'PADDY PANTSDOWN'.

Mark Oaten and Simon Hughes, Lib-Dem leadership contenders, were both recently caught in gay-sex scandals, and long ago two prominent Liberal Prime Ministers were infamous for their exploits with the fairer sex: David Lloyd George had an insatiable appetite for the ladies, while William Gladstone was notorious for stalking Victorian streets looking for prostitutes to . . . save!

Back in 1984 Keith Hampson, who was Tory MP for Leeds, was reported to be at the centre of an unintentionally hilarious case at Southwark Crown Court, all brought on because he had sunk five pints of his preferred drink, which was so strong it was known as 'brain damage'.

He was charged with 'fondling the thigh' of 'Luscious Leon', a table dancer at the Gay Theatre Club in Soho. Leon revealed himself as an undercover policeman, and Hampson was arrested.

The defence lawyer raised the issue of whether policemen had the right to appear as table dancers for the purposes of entrapment. The jury was so confused that they failed to reach a verdict and the case was dismissed.

British politicians are amateur boozers, of course, compared with the Russian bear Boris Yeltsin. His behaviour became increasingly bizarre during his years in charge at the Kremlin as rumours of excessive drinking swept through the political world.

There was plenty of evidence to suggest that he had become the puppet of alcohol. In 1994 he jumped on stage during a visit to Germany to conduct a brass band while singing and dancing. Later the same year, he failed to get off a plane during an official visit to Ireland. Russian officials announced that the President was unwell, but the common belief among journalists covering the visit was that he was drunk. He apparently did not wake up until the plane was back in Moscow, when he wanted to know the whereabouts of the Irish welcoming committee. Shortly afterwards he suffered one of several heart attacks that hurried his departure from the political scene.

In 1997, he unexpectedly and dramatically declared during a visit to Sweden that he planned to cut Russia's nuclear arsenal by one-third and work towards a total world ban on nuclear weapons. Panic-stricken

Cheers comradeski. Boris Yeltsin, always happy with a glass in his hand, toasts our Queen. Boozy Boris drank enough vodka to launch a Russian battleship.

Russian officials scrambled to correct the President, who had just inadvertently binned his country's official policy.

The following year, during a banquet with Pope John Paul II, Yeltsin toasted his 'love of Italian women', and on another occasion he played wooden spoons on the balding head of Askar Akayev, the President of Kyrgyzstan.

On an official visit to the United States everybody held their breath as Yeltsin emerged from the plane at Andrews Air Force Base and made his way very slowly down the mobile staircase. He was gripping the rails and concentrating on each step as if in a daze. Most observers assumed he was in an alcoholic fog. Russian minders did their best to block the view of the cameras recording his laboured descent, but the world saw him slipping on the last step and grabbing his wife's arm for support.

That night, in the official residence provided for him by President Bill Clinton, the Russian leader was roaring drunk, lurching from room to room in his underpants. At one point, he stumbled downstairs and accosted a secret service agent, who managed to persuade him to go back upstairs and return to the care of his personal bodyguards. Yeltsin reappeared briefly on the landing, demanding, 'Pizza! Pizza!' Finally, his bodyguards took him firmly by the arms and marched him briskly around in an effort to calm him down.

At the press conference, Yeltsin gave the world's reporters a cabaret performance that left them open-mouthed. He mocked them for having predicted that US and Russian differences over Bosnia would turn the summit into a disaster. Pointing directly at the cameras, he bellowed, 'Now, for the first time, I can tell you that *you're* a disaster!'

Clinton, standing alongside, doubled up with laughter. He slapped Boris on the back and had to wipe tears from his eyes. Still laughing, when it was his turn to come to the microphone he simply said, 'Just make sure you get the attribution right!'

The master of spin certainly did not want to get on the wrong side of the world's press.

Ah, Boris Yeltsin, politics just seemed like more fun when he was around. I bet we'll never see Vladimir Putin playing the spoons on a fellow president's head! Although, admittedly, he has been accused of spiking the odd drink or two.

Tell-tale Henry Kissinger put the boot in on his old boss Richard Nixon when he revealed that while our then Prime Minister Ted Heath was trying to contact him during the 1973 Arab–Israeli War the President was too 'loaded' to take his call.

According to official records released in 2004, Kissinger got a message to Heath that he should phone back in the morning. He told an aide that Nixon had approved a certain proposal on the crisis before adding: 'But I'm not quite sure he knew what he was approving.'

Nixon was looking for solutions to his problems in the bottom of a glass, and within a year he had resigned over the Watergate scandal.

Harry S. Truman, the President who ordered the dropping of the atom bombs on Japan, was accused of being drunk when firing one of America's most famous wartime heroes, General Douglas MacArthur.

Senator Joe McCarthy, the man who led the 'Reds-under-the-beds' communist witch-hunts of the 1950s, said that Truman was obviously 'under the influence of alcohol' when he made the decision to remove MacArthur as commander of the United Nations forces in Korea in 1951. 'Most of the President's most tragic decisions are made in the early hours of the morning,' said McCarthy, 'when his cronies have got him nice and cheerful.'

Truman liked his bourbon, but he was never regarded as a drunkard . . . unlike Senator McCarthy. How ironic that when the witch-hunter was eventually brought down by the American Senate he was exposed as a closet alcoholic.

America's fourteenth President, Franklin Pierce, was another incurable alcoholic. Asked what he planned to do when he left office, he replied: 'What is there left to do but get drunk?'

Martin Van Buren, the eighth US President, drank so heavily that he was known as 'Blue Whiskey Van'. He developed gout, brought on by his excessive wine consumption.

It was the second President, John Adams, who set the drinking fashion. He used to have a beer with his breakfast, and while in 'dry' Philadelphia he wrote the following in a letter to his wife, who was back home in more liberal Massachusetts:

I would give three guineas for a barrel of your cyder. Not one drop of it to be had here for gold, and wine is not to be had under sixty-eight dollars per gallon, and that very bad. I would give a guinea for a barrel of your beer. A small beer here is wretchedly bad. In short,

I am getting nothing that I can drink, and I believe I shall be sick from this cause alone. Rum is forty shillings a gallon, and bad water will never do in this hot climate in summer where acid liquors are necessary against infection.

George W. Bush, of course, has admitted to 'alcohol abuse', until he quit drinking at the age of forty. In his boozing days the future President of the United States was found guilty of driving while under the influence. Goodness knows what he would have got up to in the White House if he had not kicked the habit!

President Lyndon B. Johnson's favourite tipple was Scotch and soda. He used to ride around his Texas ranch in an open convertible drinking out of a large white plastic cup. Periodically, he would slow down and hold his left arm outside the car, shaking the cup and ice. A secret service agent would run up to the convertible, take the cup and go back to the station wagon that followed the President's car everywhere it went. There another agent would refill it with ice, Scotch and soda as the runner continued to trot alongside. Then the secret serviceman would take the drink back to LBJ's outstretched hand, as the President's car moved slowly forward. It became known among the agents as the 'great whiskey relay' and gave a whole new meaning to Johnson's famous political slogan, 'All the way with LBJ.'

As war hero and eighteenth US President Ulysses Grant lay dying, a priest sat praying at his bedside. At one point, Grant became unconscious. The priest sprinkled water over him, and performed some rites. A short time later, though, a doctor succeeded in reviving Grant by forcing him to take a mouthful of brandy. The priest exclaimed: 'It is Providence. It is Providence.' The doctor responded, 'No, it was the brandy.'

It should have been no surprise that a drop of alcohol had perked him up. A few years earlier at a concert it was obvious that Grant was more interested in his glasses of wine than in the music. Nevertheless, he was asked if he was enjoying the event. 'How could I?' said the tone-deaf President. 'I know only two tunes. One of them is "Yankee Doodle" . . . and the other isn't.'

When it was reported to Abraham Lincoln during the Civil War that Grant (who was then the inspirational leader of the Union forces) was consuming huge quantities of whiskey, Lincoln responded: 'It is clearly having results. Perhaps the other generals should learn from this.'

It would be impossible to leave Aussie politicians out of a book about booze! From the earliest days of the Australian parliament there was controversy over drunken incidents, including fist-fights and statesmen falling off their benches. There was an early motion to have grog banned from the parliamentary refreshment room where the Reform Club was based, but it was defeated after one of the MPs had pointed out: 'We must drink the bloody club out of debt.'

Australia's first Prime Minister, Edmund Barton, was frequently drunk at the Dispatch Box and was affectionately known throughout the country as Toby Tosspot because he was always tossing grog down his throat. He set the standards for successors such as Bob Hawke, who earned himself a place in the *Guinness Book of Records* by sinking two and a half pints of beer in just eleven seconds! 'This feat will endear me more to many of my fellow-Aussies than anything I have achieved in politics,' he said.

Glasgow-born John A. Macdonald, the first Prime Minister of Canada, was an alcoholic who was often drunk during parliamentary debates. He once vomited while at the Dispatch Box, and the leader of the opposition shouted, 'What a man to have running our country. A drunk.'

Collecting himself, Macdonald countered: 'I am sick not because of alcohol but because I am forced to listen to the rantings of my honourable opponent.'

As he cleaned himself up, he added: 'It is better for Canada to have a drunk Conservative than a sober Liberal.'

A man of quick temper, he once charged across the floor of the parliament and physically attacked a member of the opposition. As other MPs pulled him away, he said: 'I'll lick him faster than hell can scorch a feather.'

Order! Order!

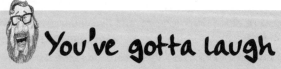# You've gotta laugh

A drunk staggers into a pub in Yorkshire and says to the landlord, 'I'd like to buy everyone in the bar a drink and have one yourself, too!'

The landlord serves drinks to everybody and they raise their glasses and toast their benefactor.

After sinking his drink, the landlord says: 'That'll be thirty-four pounds exactly.'

The drunk replies, 'Really. Well, the situation is that I don't have any money!'

The landlord is furious. He jumps over the bar and gives the drunk a good hiding before throwing him out on to the street.

At the same time the next day the same drunk comes swaying into the same pub and says to the landlord, 'I'd like to buy the whole bar a drink, and have one yourself, too.'

The landlord figures that maybe he was a little hard on the man the previous day and decides to give him the benefit of the doubt.

He serves drinks all round, including one for himself, and they all say, 'Cheers' and raise their glasses to the drunk.

'That will be thirty-six pounds, please,' says the landlord.

The drunk shrugs. 'More expensive than yesterday, and I still don't have any money!'

Now the landlord is fuming. He jumps over the bar, thumps the living daylights out of the drunk and throws him in a heap on to the street.

At the same time the next day the same drunk walks into the same pub, but before he can say anything the landlord gets in first.

'Let me guess,' he says. 'You want to buy everybody in the bar a drink and I should have one myself. Right?'

The drunk replies, 'Almost, but leave yourself out. You get terribly violent when you've had a drink!'

Hark Who's Talking About Drink

'I distrust camels and anyone else who can go a week without a drink.'
– Joe E. Lewis

'The drinks are on the house, so somebody had better go and get a ladder.'
– Spike Milligan

'The drinking is easy, it's the stopping that's hard.'
– Errol Flynn

'The problem with some people is that when they're not drunk they're sober.'
– William Butler Yeats

'Drinking in moderation equals heaven; drinking to excess equals hell.'
– Eamonn Andrews

'A good pub is one that is open.'
– Dave Allen

'The greatest drink is the next one.'
– Oliver Reed

'One more drink and I'll be under the host.'
– Dorothy Parker

'I went a whole week without a drink yesterday.'
– John Edwards

'Teaching has ruined more American novelists than drink.'
– Gore Vidal

'There's nothing to beat a good drink followed by a good drink.'
– Jeffrey Bernard

'Wine gives strength to weary men.'
– Homer

'Is there a sadder sight in the whole wide world than an empty glass that you're holding?'
– Homer Simpson

'Nothing makes me nearly as happy as talking and having a beer with my friends. And that's something everyone can do.'
– Drew Carey

'You won't find happiness at the bottom of a glass, but you'll have a good time getting there.'
– Richard Burton

'I think it's sad to drink alone, so I've bought myself a dog.'
- Max Wall

'My advice is don't drink more than you should or less than you need. Somewhere in the middle lies the perfect pint.'
- Peter O'Toole

'For we could not now take time for further search (to land our ship), our victuals being much spent, especially our Beere.'
- Captain's log on the _Mayflower_

3 Oliver Reed's TV Times

A television camera can detect somebody who's been hitting the sauce like radar picking up incoming aircraft. If you're three sheets to the wind and about to go into a TV studio, my advice is turn around and go home. It's fatal to walk out on to the set, because the lights are so flaming hot that if you've been drinking you'll suddenly feel as if all the booze inside you has been microwaved and doubled in strength.

I know my limits, so when I have a TV interview date I always take just a couple of cans of mild with me to the studio. This means I can avoid the minefield of the green room, where drink flows freely and is all too tempting, particularly for anybody nervous about appearing in front of the cameras.

The green room, the pre-show hospitality area, has been the undoing of many a television interviewee. Some crafty producers even deliberately encourage heavy raids on the bar before the show to help loosen tongues and lower inhibitions.

George Best claimed he was the victim of just that sort of nobbling before his notorious appearance on *Wogan* in 1990. He told me some time later that he had got to the studio reasonably sober but was then offered champagne by the bucket-load by production staff eager, so George said, to see him make a fool of himself. In the interests of balance, it should be said that his allegation was strenuously denied by the *Wogan* team.

Whatever the truth of how he ended up in the state that he did, he was completely out of his head by the time he came face-to-face with Terry Wogan, who had been so busy talking to other guests that he had no idea that George was in no fit state to be interviewed. 'As he came on to the set with a glazed look in his eye and a fixed grin on his face,' Terry said later, 'I knew it was going to be a hairy experience.'

The minute George started swearing and saying how much he liked 'screwing' the alarm bells rang for the host. He tried to change the subject by asking George: 'And what do you do with your time these days?'

'I screw,' said George, grinning inanely.

Mercifully, Wogan had the good sense to end the interview right there. 'Ladies and gentlemen, George Best,' he said, ignoring the fact that his show was now under-running by at least ten minutes.

He got George off camera as soon as he could, but the damage had been done. It was front-page news the next day, and George was hounded for weeks by reporters wanting to ask him about his drink problem. 'It was', George told me, 'one of the lowest points of my life.'

It was not funny for him, but it provided the kind of on-the-edge television that producers crave. And, let's be honest, it makes riveting viewing.

However, George's TV performances were small beer compared to those of a man who became a legless legend in his own lifetime: the one and only Oliver Reed.

For some reason which no one was ever able to fathom, Ollie seemed obsessed with talking about his private parts. But when he was drunk he liked to go further, continually wanting to show off his 'todger', as he called it. Once, on Des O'Connor's chat show, Ollie mentioned that he had an eagle's head tattooed on his shoulder, which seemed innocent enough. Unfortunately, the host did not realise that, as a follow-up, Reed

Oliver Reed failed to get the James Bond role because he was too often shaken *AND* stirred.

would inevitably ask: 'Want to see where it's perched?' Those foolish enough to say 'yes' would be treated to the sight of Reed unzipping his trousers and revealing the pair of eagle's claws that adorned his man-hood. Des had to use considerable persuasion to stop Ollie doing just that on national TV.

It might not have mattered too much anyway. Michael Parkinson and actress Elaine Stritch got to see what all the fuss was about when they appeared with Ollie on a radio programme. He arrived wearing just a pair of wellington boots. Elaine looked him up and down and said: 'To be honest, I've seen bigger and better.'

On another occasion, Ollie arrived next to legless on the Patrick Kielty chat show in Belfast. The very first question ('How long have you been in Ireland?') was greeted with: 'How long's your knob?'

But his most infamous televised drunken performance came on the *Aspel and Co.* show, when he came stumbling on to the set carrying a quart glass of orange juice. It soon became clear that he had been drinking something much stronger in the green room. Michael Aspel did his best to get some coherent comments from him, but Ollie was too far gone to make much sense. Yet he was alert enough to correct the host when he said that Ollie had once drunk one hundred and four pints in twenty-four hours. Not being one to boast, Ollie admitted, 'It was forty-eight hours.'

Fellow-guest Clive James asked him: 'Why do you drink?'

'Because, dear boy,' replied Ollie, 'the most wonderful people I have ever met in my life are in pubs.'

He then staggered across the floor to where the studio orchestra was stationed and demanded that they play the Troggs hit 'Wild Thing', which he proceeded to perform in a toe-curlingly embarrassing way.

The producers on *The Word* were cruel to him, secretly filming him getting drunk in his dressing-room before coming on to the set and giving another appalling rendering of 'Wild Thing'. Bumping into the show's presenter Mark Lamarr backstage, he asked: 'Who the f*** are you? The f****** warm-up man?'

His two weirdest television performances were seen by only a handful of viewers. First, there was an obscure Channel 4 show called *After Dark* in which intellectuals debated off-beat subjects long after midnight. There were seven stone-cold-sober eggheads and, right in the middle of them, Ollie as pissed as a newt. He kept interrupting highbrow arguments with slurred asides, and gave each of his fellow-panellists unflattering nicknames ('Big Tits' . . . 'Flash Guy' . . . 'F*** Face'). He reached his nadir when he twice used the unmentionable 'c' word. The eggheads continued to talk around him as if he didn't exist, but that really infuriated Ollie, who resorted to his favourite theme, threatening to put his 'plonker' (his description) on the table for discussion. It ended in a shambles when Ollie suddenly stood up and announced: 'I'm going for a slash.' To everyone's evident relief, he left the set before doing so.

Then came one of the most bizarre television interviews ever screened. It was called *Oliver Reed in the Barber's Chair*, a segment in a short-lived London Weekend Television series with the emphasis on European culture and aimed at a late-night audience. Ollie sat in a barber's chair dressed, for some obscure reason, as Father Christmas. A French barber proceeded to trim his false beard, then gave him a real haircut and shaved off his huge moustache, all the time interviewing Ollie in a heavy Gallic accent.

Throughout the half-hour show, Ollie continually insulted the barber, calling him 'you f****** stupid French frog' and other less flattering names. He invited one of the camera crew to have a fight, and kept pulling strange faces as he looked at himself in the mirror. At one stage he punched a hand-held mirror so hard that it shattered, and demanded heavy make-up because he hated the way he looked after he had been shorn. At the close of the show he got the barber in a bear hug and very nearly squashed the life out of him.

Someone has had the foresight to put this amazing performance on YouTube. Catch it if you can. I guarantee you will not believe your eyes.

Ollie found it more difficult to be accepted on network television in the United States, where one swear word on air can have you on the next plane out. Because of his reputation for being dangerous, he found invitations for live chat shows hard to come by, particularly after being interviewed by hostess Rona Barrett. She objected to him smoking on set. Instead of stubbing out his cigarette, Ollie pushed it into his mouth and swallowed it!

David Letterman, one of the top chat-show hosts, had the guts to interview him, but the director kept his finger close to the 'cut to commercials' button throughout. Whenever it was sensed Ollie was going to become boisterous or crude, viewers suddenly found themselves watching advertisements.

Oliver Reed was an exceptionally gifted actor who could bring brooding menace or touching sensitivity to the screen. I just wonder how good he might have been but for his dependence on drink. He would have made a great James Bond, a role he very nearly landed until his drinking exploits gave him an image too far removed from Ian Fleming's hero.

Sadly, Ollie was too often shaken *and* stirred.

From a big drinker to a little one: Danny DeVito, a tiny man compared to the muscular Oliver Reed, but by all accounts one with a similar appetite for booze.

He shocked America by taking the piss out of President George W. Bush while appearing to be sloshed on a coast-to-coast TV show in the spring of 2007.

Diminutive Danny managed to call Bush 'Numb Nuts' before they got to work on him with the bleeper, while the show's host Barbara Walters tried to hide her mixture of despair and disgust at his on-screen behaviour.

What they couldn't bleep was Danny pulling village-idiot faces as he impersonated the President. And he slurringly managed to share with the nation the revelation that he and his wife, *Cheers* actress Rhea Perlman, had made love in every conceivable position in the Abraham Lincoln Room during an overnight stay at the White House when Bill Clinton was into his second term.

Danny revealed that he had come to the studio straight from an all-night drinking session with heart-throb actor George Clooney. 'I knew it was the last seven limoncellos that were going to get me,' he said about his favourite drink, a lethal Italian liqueur.

His send-up of George Bush and his 'tired and emotional' state brought Danny huge publicity, with his comments about limoncello receiving special attention. A few weeks later, the cheeky little so-and-so announced that he was launching his own brand of the now-famous liqueur. Which makes you think that maybe he wasn't so drunk and stupid after all.

The experienced television presenter Bill Grundy had made a name for himself in the sixties, when, among other things, he had introduced the Beatles during their debut on Granada TV. But a decade later, times had changed, and pop groups were no longer polite young men in suits.

In one of the most notorious shows in British TV history, the Sex Pistols would prove a bridge too far for Grundy's casual interviewing technique. The pioneering punk group, then barely known, were a last-minute booking for the *Thames Television Today* show on 1 December 1976, after Freddie Mercury's Queen had pulled out.

The previous year, Bill had been forgiven for being drunk on air when presenting a programme on the Derby from Epsom. His namesake Grundy had been first past the post, so his bosses could understand why he had piled into the champagne.

But he could find no excuses the day he locked horns with the Pistols, who were peddling their new brand of music and were clearly out to shock. They arrived at the studio with a full entourage, and this is how Bill, with help from the autocue, introduced the band and their hangers-on: 'Left to right, we have: Johnny Rotten, Steve Jones, Glen Matlock and Paul Cook. And standing behind the Pistols are their supporters from the Bromley Contingent, Siouxsie Sioux, Steve Severin, Simon Barker and Simone.'

So far, so good. Then Bill started the interview that was to make headlines across the country the next morning. Thanks to a pal of mine who used to work at Thames, I can give you the full, verbatim transcript:

GRUNDY *(To camera)*: They are punk rockers. The new craze, they tell me. Their heroes? Not the nice, clean Rolling Stones. You see they are as drunk as I am. The Stones are clean by comparison. This is a group called the Sex Pistols, and I am surrounded by all of them . . .

JONES *(Reading the autocue over Grundy's shoulder)*: In action!

GRUNDY *(Glaring at Jones)*: Now just let's see the Sex Pistols in action. Come on kids . . .

(Run film of the Sex Pistols, back to Grundy.)

GRUNDY: I am told that your group have received forty thousand pounds from a record company. Doesn't that seem, er, to be slightly opposed to your anti-materialistic view of life?

MATLOCK: No, the more the merrier.

GRUNDY: Really?

MATLOCK: Oh yeah.

GRUNDY: Well, tell me more then.

JONES: We've fuckin' spent it, ain't we?

GRUNDY: I don't know, have you?

MATLOCK: Yeah, it's all gone.

GRUNDY: Really? Gone where?

JONES: Down the boozer.

GRUNDY: Really? Good Lord! Now I want to know one thing . . .

MATLOCK: What?

GRUNDY: Are you serious or are you just having me on, trying to make me laugh?

MATLOCK: No, it's all gone. Gone.

GRUNDY: Really?

MATLOCK: Yeah.

GRUNDY: No, but I mean about what you're doing. This so-called music. You're serious about it?

MATLOCK: Oh yeah.

GRUNDY: You are really serious?

MATLOCK: I've told you. Yeah.

GRUNDY: Beethoven, Mozart, Bach and Brahms have all died . . .

ROTTEN: They're all heroes of ours, ain't they?

GRUNDY: Really . . . what? *(Now looking intently at Rotten)* What were you saying, sir?

ROTTEN: They're wonderful people.

GRUNDY: Are they?

ROTTEN: Oh yes! They really turn us on.

JONES: But they're all dead geezers!

GRUNDY: Well, suppose they turn other people on?

ROTTEN *(Aside)*: That's just their tough shit.

GRUNDY: It's what? What was that you said?

ROTTEN: Nothing. A rude word. Next question.

GRUNDY: No, no, what was the rude word?

ROTTEN: 'Shit'.

GRUNDY: Was it *really*. Good heavens, you frighten me to death.

ROTTEN: Oh all right, Siegfried . . .

GRUNDY *(Turning to the hangers-on at the back)*: What about you girls behind?

MATLOCK: He's like yer dad, inni, this geezer?

GRUNDY: Are you, er . . .

MATLOCK: Or your granddad, more like.

GRUNDY *(To nineteen-year-old Sioux)*: Are you worried, or are you just enjoying yourself?

SIOUX: Enjoying meself.

GRUNDY: Are you?

SIOUX: Yeah.

GRUNDY: Ah, that's what I thought you were doing.

SIOUX: I always wanted to meet you.

GRUNDY: Did you really?

SIOUX: Yeah.

GRUNDY: We'll meet afterwards, shall we?

JONES: You dirty sod. You dirty old man!

GRUNDY: Well, keep going, chief, keep going. Go on, you've got another five seconds. Say something outrageous.

JONES: You dirty bastard!

GRUNDY: Go on, again.

JONES: You dirty fucker! *(The group fall about laughing.)*

GRUNDY: What a clever boy!

JONES: What a fucking rotter.

GRUNDY: Well, that's it for tonight. The other rocker Eamonn [Andrews] will be back tomorrow. I'll be seeing you soon. I hope I'm not seeing you lot [the band] again. From me, though, goodnight.

As the closing credits rolled, the Pistols were dancing to the signature tune (which was later incorporated in the song 'Where's Bill Grundy Now?'). Grundy was heard to say aloud to himself, 'Oh shit.'

The Thames Television switchboard was jammed with calls from complaining viewers, split between disgust over the behaviour of the band and outrage over the seemingly provocative interviewing of Grundy.

It was virtually the end of his career as a front-line presenter, whereas overnight the Sex Pistols became one of the best-known groups in the land. The *Daily Mirror* ran the story as a front-page lead with the roaring headline: 'THE FILTH AND THE FURY'. The Pistols could not have bought a tenth of the publicity. Bill Grundy had made their day, punk.

Put Charlotte Church and Johnny Vegas together and you could have an explosive cocktail, and so it proved when the 'Voice of an Angel'-turned-rock-diva had the apparently pissed, larger-than-life comedian as a guest on her chat show.

There was a time when you thought butter would not melt in Charlotte's mouth, but she now has a nice line in barbed comments that hit home like red-hot needles. On this occasion, though, more direct action was necessary. The breaking point came when Vegas claimed that he had sh*gged Charlotte's grandmother. 'Shut the f*** up,' she screamed, accompanying her instruction with a right-hander of which her countryman Joe Calzaghe would have been proud.

Another volatile pop star is Liam Gallagher. He seems to want to do more fighting than his fellow-Mancunian Ricky 'The Hit Man' Hatton, and has been filmed repeatedly being aggressive with photographers and in less than full control of himself on stage and at awards ceremonies.

One incident I would love to have seen happened in 2006, when Gallagher and Paul Gascoigne reportedly had a drunken brawl at London's posh Groucho Club. It apparently ended with Gallagher setting off a fire extinguisher in Gazza's face.

Later the same year, according to newspaper reports, Liam rang Virgin

Radio on the *Who's Calling Christian O'Connell?* show, where the hook is that you can win £10,000 for charity.

The switchboard refused to believe that it was the real Liam Gallagher, and kept cutting him off. He apparently persisted for three hours, getting steadily more drunk and abusive. At one stage he was alleged to have threatened: 'I'm gonna come down there and rip Christian O'Connell's f****** head off.'

He finally convinced the station's bosses that he was the one and only Liam Gallagher by sending them a mobile phone image of himself. They then made the mistake of putting him live on air: he was quickly off again after filling the airwaves with four-letter words.

One thing's for sure, Liam is not in an oasis of calm.

British pop stars who consider themselves heavy drinkers would not have lived with the Godfather of Soul, James Brown. Somehow, he managed to survive to seventy-four despite a rip-roaring lifestyle that would have worn out most people years earlier.

He was arrested and jailed several times for misuse of alcohol, drugs, guns and vehicles, as well as for domestic disputes with his four wives. Despite all that, Brown toured relentlessly throughout his life, and his energetic, all-action dancing performances earned him the nickname 'The Hardest-Working Man in Showbusiness'.

In 1988, Brown's personal life came crashing down when he was accused by his wife of assault and battery. A year trying to cope with legal and personal troubles boiled up into an amazing climax when he led the police on an interstate car chase after allegedly threatening people with a handgun. The dramatic episode ended in a six-year prison sentence that many felt was excessive; he was eventually paroled after serving two years.

This would have finished most performers in the fickle music industry, but not the unique James Brown. He came rocking back and was lifted to iconic status by his army of followers.

He always seemed to be walking hand-in-hand with controversy. After being accused of threatening another of his wives with a lead pipe and a gun, he gave an astonishing live television interview while out on bail.

Viewers looked on open-mouthed as he sang many of his replies ('This is a man's world' . . . 'I f-e-e-l good'). He also rambled on about how well he made love and almost in the same breath talked about the Second Coming.

Only the Godfather of Soul could have got away with it.

American Idol judge Paula Abdul has had millions of viewers in the States wondering whether she has been hitting the bottle. In one breakfast-time interview from New York City she could hardly keep still, and she was giggly and incoherent throughout the questioning.

And on one of the shows – sitting alongside Simon Cowell on the judging bench – she came out with this mouthful: 'What did you tell me, Simon? What did you tell me? Simon gave me advice and said on *The X Factor* he always refers to a fortune cookie and says the moth who finds the melon finds the cornflake, always finds the melon and one of you didn't pick the right fortune.'

Are these the words of a sober judge? The jury is out.

Supremes singer Diana Ross was charged with drink-driving in December 2003. The local TV company was tipped off and rushed a crew to the police station. 'Were you drunk, Diana?' asked a reporter. 'No, I was just looking for the video store and got lost and confused,' the diva said. Later, the arresting police officer reported: 'Miss Ross was driving erratically and I ordered her to pull over. When I asked her to stand on one leg and count to ten she fell over, and started to laugh.'

Diana was found to have a blood-alcohol level more than

double the legal limit. She was found guilty and sentenced to twenty-four hours in an Arizona jail. It seems she didn't have a leg to stand on.

Watching a much younger singer than Diana Ross – Britney Spears – come apart at the seams through alcohol and drug abuse is like witnessing a slow-motion car crash. You can do nothing to stop it, but you can scarcely bring yourself to look away.

She has appeared time and again on camera in an obviously drunken state, and it was heart-wrenching to hear her slur: 'I feel I've lost out on life . . . on the whole living thing.'

I'm from the generation that cannot begin to understand why young girls are hitting the bottle. In my younger days (makes me sound like an old fart, I know) no women, and certainly no girls, went near a pub without a male escort. Now too many glamorous role models seem happy to appear smashed in public.

As I try to stress all the way through this book, drinking to excess is neither fun nor sensible. End of lecture.

The following is a true story, but I will change the name to protect the guilty.

An American beauty queen – let's call her Miss Planet – had just collected her title and told the television interviewer: 'I will campaign for world peace and against people who drink and drive.' A few hours later she was arrested for drink-driving after going through a red light, and when interviewed at the police station she told the duty sergeant in a slurred voice: 'And I don't give a shit about world peace either.'

New rhyming slang entered the vocabulary when Reginald Bosanquet was reading the ITN news bulletins: 'completely broadcastered' (plastered).

Reggie was a brilliant newsreader, but often seemed to slur his words. The joke was that he should have been called Reginald Beaujolais.

The son of the England Test cricketer who invented the googly, Bosanquet admitted that he liked a drink or three but insisted that his slurred speech was due to a medical condition. Whatever the truth, he made some spectacular gaffes, seemed in the George Bush league for mispronunciations and often struggled with difficult place names.

Reggie and Anna Ford were a popular team, and as a proud English gentleman he would go out of his way to be gallant to her. Without telling Anna, he found out her mother's date of birth, and at the end of one news bulletin wished the lady a very happy birthday. It was left to a tearful Anna to tell him that her mother had died some time previously.

Following his retirement, he was the controversial choice as the Lord Rector of Glasgow University, a post he held for four years from 1980. Those who opposed him thought, like so many viewers, that he had a drink problem. And they had good reason.

The man who had read thousands of news items filled the headlines himself when he turned up late for an official reception at the university obviously the worse for wear. He insulted several VIP guests, including the Lord Provost of Glasgow. It was said you could almost hear the ITN gong sounding '*boing!*' with every slurred word he uttered.

Here's another tale of the unexpected from the 'you'll never believe it' department. I could not get it past the lawyers by using the real name of the celebrity involved, so for the purposes of relating the story I am going to call him Harry Smith.

This well-known star of the stage and screen was booked for a guest walk-on appearance on a *This Is Your Life* tribute to another prominent celebrity. It was back in the days of Eamonn Andrews being in charge of the big red book, when many of the shows went out live.

At the rehearsal, which took place two hours before the show proper, he walked on, said his piece perfectly to the stand-in subject and then strode elegantly to his seat on the set. No problem.

Unfortunately, he then headed to a nearby pub before returning to continue his drinking in the studio green room. The researchers backstage were too busy to notice that our man was getting progressively more pie-eyed. Before long, he was being steered to the wings to await his cue from Eamonn.

'And here's a voice from your past that you may recall,' said the host.

The guest's pre-recorded voice-over was heard by the subject in the chair and the viewers sitting at home.

'Yes,' said Eamonn, 'he's here tonight, you haven't seen him for fifteen years . . . Harry Smith.'

By now pissed out of his head, Harry stood frozen to the spot until given a nudge in the back by the floor manager. He entered stage left, weaved all the way across the back of the set, and exited stage right.

Neither the subject nor Eamonn got to say a word to him.

Being the consummate professional, Eamonn ad-libbed: 'Yes, that was Harry, and he will be in a hurry to see you after the show.'

Meantime, Harry was staggering back towards the green room and bumped into the chauffeur who had earlier picked him up and delivered him to the studio. He was driven back to his home without speaking to a soul, and woke up the next morning wondering when he was due to go on *This Is Your Life*.

Beautiful French-Canadian reporter Anne-Marie Losique didn't quite get the interview she expected when she went to Los Angeles for a one-to-one chat with actor Ben Affleck. He sat her on his lap and fondled her intimately throughout the interview, while suggesting 'get your titties out'.

There were allegations he had been hitting the bottle as he made French-accented come-ons, using such lines as: 'Why are you not showing more cleavage?' and 'You should have that rack on display.'

The large-bosomed Ms Losique giggled all the way through the one-sided chat, asking few questions and concentrating on trying to control big Ben's hands.

I wonder if I should do the same thing the next time I'm on Parky?

One of the saddest drunks on television in recent years has been *Baywatch* and *Knight Rider* star David Hasselhoff. In the UK we guessed he was still having problems beating the bottle when he appeared to be rat-arsed during a 2006 breakfast-time appearance on GMTV. Hundreds of viewers rang the station to complain about his performance.

He slurred his words and at times seemed half asleep as he sat alongside presenter Jenni Falconer, occasionally making suggestive comments to her that she tried to ignore while reading the autocue.

The Hoff struggled to pronounce the name of his co-star Adam Sandler ('Sanglier') while plugging their latest film, and then got a link embarrassingly wrong. Finally, he was hopelessly out of sync while trying to mime to one of his records.

His spokesperson put out a statement that he was not drunk but just tired after too heavy a workload. It might have done him a favour to admit that he still had the problem he had been trying to fight for several years. Then he could have avoided the terrible humiliation of being filmed drunk out of his head by his daughter a few months later.

She shot it to try to convince him to get treatment, not knowing that the film would be hijacked and released for worldwide viewing. But at least it brought home the horrors of excessive drinking, and everybody joined together in hoping the Hoff would use the awful exposure as motivation to get himself sorted out.

We are much more relaxed over the use of the f-word on television here than in America, where swearing can bring down the wrath of the Bible Belt.

Two beer guts that could tell a tale or three! I'm with Johnny Vegas on the set of *The Virgin of Liverpool*. That's one thing Johnny didn't call Charlotte Church when blotto on her TV show.

Actor Bruce Willis was relaxing as a spectator at a basketball game in May 2007 when he was interviewed by a television reporter. Seemingly intoxicated by the excitement of the match, Bruce let slip the f-word on the national network. The telephone lines went into meltdown with complaints, and the TV company had to issue an official apology.

In case you're wondering, Gordon Ramsay can get away with his *F-Word* show on US television because he appears on cable and subscription channels, where the rules are much less rigid. He would be roasted if he let rip with his swearing on network TV.

Other celebrities have been caught out while watching sport from the sidelines in the States after indulging in a little liquid refreshment. Quarterback legend Joe Namath is probably the biggest idol in American football history (O.J. Simpson used to share that accolade, but he is not such a hero any more, as you can imagine). Old Joe was minding his business watching his former team the New York Jets in action when a roving female TV reporter with a microphone and accompanying camera moved in on him for an unscheduled chat.

Oh dear. Joe really should have been left alone to enjoy the game. He slurred a lot of nonsense about the future of the Jets, then confirmed that he was not quite with it when he kept asking for a kiss from the reporter.

One of the commentators said: 'It's good to see Joe happy.'

'Yes,' agreed his colleague. 'Very, very happy.'

Delia Smith, Queen of the Kitchen, cooked up a storm in her role as Norwich City director in February 2005. She grabbed the microphone on the pitch at half-time with the Canaries drawing with Manchester City and yelled at the fans: 'Where are you? Where are you? Let's be having you. Come on.'

The consensus of opinion was that Delia had been at either the cooking sherry or the boardroom champagne, but she insisted she was simply speaking with passion and from the heart. It was just her bad luck that Sky cameras were recording her live and she came across as a shrill football fanatic rather than the demure Delia we all know and love.

Have there ever been so many drunks on live television at any one time as during the coverage of England's Ashes victory celebrations in the summer of 2006?

Freddie Flintoff, in particular, was out of his tree, but the player who deserved the 'Most Sozzled' award was fast bowler Matthew Hoggard. When the squad arrived in a legless state at Downing Street to meet the Prime Minister he called Tony Blair 'a knob', which many might consider fair comment, but it's hardly the done thing to say it to the host of an official reception. Even David Cameron didn't get that insulting during their days battling at the Dispatch Box.

But the team certainly had good reason to celebrate. Their efforts the previous day had been watched by 7.4 million people on Channel 4, and for the first time in decades cricket seemed more important to a lot of people than footie.

Freddie Flintoff and Matthew Hoggard will certainly drink to that.

Robin Williams won the hearts of Americans when he announced he was going into rehab after admitting he had an alcohol abuse problem after twenty years of sobriety.

A few months later, having beaten the bottle, Robin was invited to the 2004 San Francisco Film Festival to receive a special award for his acting career.

Making his acceptance speech, he thanked the sponsors: a drinks company. 'Just out of rehab,' he told the black-tie audience, 'it's always good to go to a place where there's a bottle of vodka on every table!'

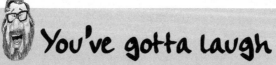

You've gotta laugh

As he sits sinking pints in a local pub a man is propositioned by a gorgeous woman who had been eyeing him up for some time. He politely explains that he has a wife at home and cannot take her up on her kind offer, but he still invites her to join him for a drink or three.

After an hour of drinking and enjoying each other's company she again asks him to come back to her place. With his defences weakened, this time he accepts the invitation.

On the way out of the bar he grabs a piece of chalk by the side of the dartboard and puts it in his coat pocket. The woman gives him a strange look but thinks nothing more of it.

Following an intimate time at her place the man decides he should take a cab home. As he reaches the front door of his house on wobbly legs he takes the chalk out of his pocket and puts it behind his ear.

His wife is waiting up for him, and gives him the third degree. 'What time do you call this?' she says. 'Where the hell have you been?'

He giggles stupidly and flippantly confesses: 'If you must know, I met a gorgeous young woman in a bar and we have been back at her place for the last two hours making wild, passionate love.'

'You must think I'm stupid,' says his wife. 'I know you've been out playing darts with your mates again. You've still got the bloody chalk behind your ear, you idiot!'

Hark Who's Talking About Drink

'I've done more than my fair share in trying to boost the American economy by drinking as much as I possibly can. But do I get any gratitude?'
– Bing Crosby

'I saw a notice that said, "Drink Canada Dry" and I've just started.'
– Brendan Behan

'A drunk was in front of a judge. The judge says, "You've been brought here for drinking." The drunk says, "OK, let's get started."'
– Henry Youngman

'Not everyone who drinks is a poet. Some of us drink because we're not poets.'
– Dudley Moore

'Actually, it only takes one drink to get me loaded. Trouble is, I can't remember if it's the thirteenth or fourteenth.'
– George Burns

'No animal ever invented anything as bad as drunkenness or as good as alcohol.'
– G.K. Chesterton

'You can't be considered a real country unless you have a beer and an airline. It also helps if you have some kind of football team, or some nuclear weapons. But, at the very least, you need a beer.'
– Frank Zappa

'American beer is a lot like making love in a rowing boat . . . it's f****** close to water.'
– Eric Idle

'British beer is so warm you could take a shower in it.'
– Sammy Davis Jnr

'The day I stop drinking is the day I stop breathing, and you will be surprised to learn that the day I stop breathing is the day I stop drinking.'
– Jeffrey Bernard

'I drink to forget, but can't remember what I'm trying to forget.'
– Eric Morecambe

'My wife drove me to drink . . . when she dropped me off at the Coach and Horses.'
– John Edwards

'The two words I hate most in all this world . . . "Last orders!"'
– **Dickie Henderson**

'I said to the barman, "Give me a pint and make it snappy." He served me a glass with a mousetrap in it.'
– **Max Miller**

'Laugh and the world laughs with you. Cry and you cry alone. Drink and you couldn't care less.'
– **Tommy Cooper**

'I wouldn't say he's tight, but when he walks into a pub he has his hands so deep in his pockets that he can feel his knees.'
– **Les Dawson**

'My friends felt I was drinking too heavily and encouraged me to join the AA. Best thing I ever did. They are always there to give me a start if I get stuck in the pub car park.'
– **Bob Monkhouse**

4 The Rat-arsed Pack

Frank Sinatra and his Rat Pack turned boozing into something of an art form, and were considered Scotch-on-the-rocks cool. Mind you, I would have backed our Mersey Pack to have matched them in the drinking stakes, and certainly to have beaten them for comedy. We could hold a tune, too. I'm talking Ken Dodd, Stan Boardman, Geoff Hughes, Tom O'Connor, and myself on banjo, with Frank Carson as our sort of Irish Sammy Davis Jnr!

I am jesting, of course. Nobody could hold a candle, certainly not one burned at both ends, to the original Rat Pack; and this may surprise you, this was *before* Sammy Davis and Dean Martin became members. It all started back in 1955 when the originator of the Rat Pack – Humphrey Bogart – invited a dozen pals to join him on a trip to Las Vegas to catch Noël Coward's opening show at the Desert Inn.

Among them were Sinatra, David Niven, Spencer Tracy, song-writer Jimmy van Heusen (who had no fewer than seventy-six songs recorded by Frank), producer Sid Luft, restaurateur Mike Romanoff, and lady rats Lauren Bacall, Angie Dickinson, Katharine Hepburn and Judy 'Mrs Luft' Garland. These were the founder members. They earned their Rat Pack label when Bacall – Mrs Bogart – took a panoramic view of them after a night of heavy drinking and said: 'You look like a goddamn rat pack.'

Bogart was the main motivator in keeping the gag and the gang going, making Sinatra the 'Pack Master' and designing a coat of arms – a rat gnawing on a human hand – with the motto: 'Never rat on a rat.'

When Bogie succumbed to cancer in 1957, Sinatra waited a respectful couple of years before recruiting new members to the Pack. They included Martin, Davis Jnr, comedian Joey Bishop, and English actor Peter Lawford, the brother-in-law of John F. Kennedy, who was then a Massachusetts senator with his eye on the White House. Among the new lady rats were Juliet Prowse and Shirley MacLaine.

Sinatra preferred the group to be called 'The Clan', 'The Summit' or 'The Board', with him as Chairman, of course. But the media had hooked on to the Rat Pack so that was the name that stuck, and to this day spawns packs of imitators.

The original Rat Pack was very much a vehicle for fun (and a reason for a good drink), but Sinatra shrewdly saw the commercial possibilities. Along with Martin and Davis Jnr, he turned Las Vegas into a goldmine with their hugely popular hotel cabaret performances, and the Pack also produced a flurry of so-so films, including *Some Came Running*, *Ocean's Eleven*, *Sergeants 3*, *4 for Texas*, *Robin and the Seven Hoods* and *Marriage on the Rocks*.

One thing's for sure, you cannot compile a collection of booze stories without reference to the Rat Pack. Some of the tales that follow are not directly drink related, but it's odds on that a few shandies were consumed by the perpetrators soon afterwards, if not before. And, anyway, as Sinatra would say, I'm here to entertain you!

Dean Martin had the reputation for being the Rat Pack drunk, but much of it was an act. That 'whiskey' he was drinking on stage was usually just plain old apple juice.

A lot of critics said that he couldn't act his way out of a paper bag, but he was good enough to convince most people that he was drunk through much of his career. He used to come on stage in his solo act with a cigarette and a full glass, acknowledging the applause as he walked unsteadily to the centre of the stage. Then, still not having said a word or sung a note, he would meander to his pianist and stage whisper: 'How long have I been on?'

But the real king drinker of the Rat Pack was The Guv'nor, Frank Sinatra. He always claimed that his best friend was Jack Daniel's, and when he was buried at the close of one of the great show-business lives in 1998, a bottle was placed in the casket with him.

Sinatra had dozens of great quips about his love of alcohol. Try these for size:

'I feel sorry for people who don't drink. When they wake up in the morning, that's as good as they're going to feel all day.'

'Basically, I'm for anything that gets you through the night – be it prayer, tranquillisers or a bottle of Jack Daniel's.'

'Alcohol may be man's worst enemy, but the Bible says, "Love your enemy."'

'I said I was thirsty, not dirty!' (To a barman who added water to his Jack Daniel's, which he always drank neat.)

His favourite toast to anybody younger, while raising a glass of bourbon, was: 'May you live to be a hundred, and may the last voice you hear be mine.'

Sinatra failed to make the ton, dying at the age of eighty-two, but if you believe all you hear and read, it was something of a miracle he made it that far.

This is how he put it: 'If I'd drunk all the drinks and drilled all the broads I'm supposed to have done then I'd now be talking to you from a jar in the Harvard medical school.'

Sinatra was shown how to drink (*really* drink) by the master, Humphrey Bogart, the man who introduced him to Jack Daniel's. It was Bogie's boast that he could drink anybody under the table, and among his scalps were famous Hollywood hard drinkers Errol Flynn, John Huston, Richard Burton and David Niven.

Once, after an all-night drinking session, he found himself staggering through unfamiliar Hollywood back streets. He smelled the aroma of frying bacon and eggs, stumbled down a garden path, and looked in through the kitchen window.

A woman stood cooking the family breakfast, and let out a scream when she saw the face of the Hollywood screen idol grinning inanely back at her.

'What the hell's up?' shouted her husband from the dining room.

'It's Humphrey Bogart!'

'What about him?' her husband asked.

'He's in our garden.'

The husband checked, realised that his wife was not seeing things and invited in the dishevelled Bogart.

They told the newspapers the next day that they'd had the breakfast of a lifetime with the film legend, who had entertained them with Hollywood stories while wolfing down bacon, eggs and coffee.

When approached and asked if the story was true, Bogie said: 'Sure. Best breakfast I ever had. Damned if I know how I got there, though!'

Many celebrities not wanting to be recognised when going out put on a wig to help disguise themselves. Evidence that Frank Sinatra was not one of them came from British comedian Michael Bentine.

He revealed on a television chat show how he and his wife, Clementina, had been taken to Mike Romanoff's Hollywood restaurant, a famous watering hole for celebrities:

While our host left us at the bar to see about our table, my wife got chatting to a slim, elderly bald man sitting alone on a stool. She asked him if any film stars came in, and he replied: 'Well, a few faces do come in from time to time. I'm sure if you're patient you'll see some. Just stick around.'

Clemmy could not help but notice that the man had an empty lipstick holder on his little finger. He explained that he had caught his finger in the car door, and this protected it perfectly. We were then summoned to join our host, and my wife explained how the man at the bar had been so pleasant and that he said that she would be pretty certain to see some film stars.

Our host looked towards the bar, and said very slowly and with great relish: 'Well, honey, you've just met the biggest one of them all. That's Frank Sinatra.'

Yes, while many stars who want to go incognito put on wigs, Sinatra used to take his off and suddenly age twenty years!

Much of the Rat Pack humour on stage used to revolve around Sammy Davis Jnr and the fact that he was black. In one show Dean Martin, pretending to be very drunk, picked up the diminutive Davis and handed him across to Sinatra: 'Congratulations,' he said. 'Here's your award from the National Association for the Advancement of Colored People.'

Sammy went along with the gag and humbly told the audience: 'I'm so fortunate that I can get insulted in places where the average Negro can never hope to get insulted.'

This may seem cringe-making in this politically correct age, but Sinatra was in fact a huge force behind the scenes in the battle for Civil Rights in the 1960s. If any hotel or club refused to allow Sammy in through the front door (common in those days for black people in the USA), The Guv'nor would refuse to do his show.

Asked on a chat show why he drank so much, Dean Martin told the host with his trademark slurred voice: 'To help me get through the ordeal of shows like this.' He then looked straight into the camera and said: 'When I arrived there was enough hooch in the hospitality room to sink the *Titanic*. I've seen to it there's now not enough left to rock a rowing boat.'

It was all part and parcel of the Martin act. When he launched the *Dean Martin Show* on network television he sat at the on-stage bar and told viewers: 'This is going to be a family show, folks, the kind of show where a man can take his wife and kids, his father and mother and sit around in a bar and watch.'

It was an opening line that brought him huge criticism from Middle America, where claims were made that he was encouraging kids to drink.

In his next show he feigned a more responsible attitude, saying: 'Folks, I'm pleading with you . . . if you drink, don't drive. Don't even putt!'

Before his showbusiness career took off, Martin worked as a professional card dealer and gambler. When he became established as an actor and singer, he said: 'Don't nobody tell me that acting is hard. Anyone who says it is has never had to stand on his feet all day dealing blackjack.'

He may have been able to count at the card table, but he appeared to have got lost in a maze of mathematics when struggling to make a living as a nightclub singer. He cut his band-leader in on 10 per cent of his earnings, his manager took 25 per cent, he paid back 10 per cent of his advance to record company MCA, paid 35 per cent to a friend who had loaned him some money to pay off his gambling debts, and 20 per cent to Lou Costello for bailing him out on one occasion. After a few other percentages had come to light, his accountant told him: 'You are now giving away 110 per cent of your earnings!' Unsurprisingly, Deano had to declare himself bankrupt. Then he met comedian Jerry Lewis in a nightclub, and the rest is history.

It was suggested that comedians making jokes at the expense of Sinatra were taking their life in their hands. In his act, New Yorker Richard Belzer told a joke about Old Blue Eyes and then fell on the floor pretending he had been shot.

Don Rickles was one of the few comics allowed to get away with taking the mickey out of Frank without getting a visit from his dodgy associates. When Sinatra once entered a club during one of his stand-up routines, Rickles ad-libbed: 'Come right on in, Frankie, and make yourself at home. Hit somebody.'

Jackie Mason, the razor-tongued rabbi-turned-comedian, made jokes about Sinatra's surprise marriage to the much younger Mia Farrow, whose close-cut hair gave her an androgynous appearance ('I always knew he would be attracted to a boy,' miaowed his previous wife, Ava Gardner).

Mason received life-threatening phone calls and was warned to drop the jokes from his routine. He kept them in and three shots were fired into his hotel room. The local sheriff was called in but nothing was found to link Sinatra with the shooting.

Appearing in Miami shortly afterwards, Mason joked: 'I don't know who it was that tried to shoot me. All I know is that just after the third bullet I heard someone singing: "Doobie, doobie, do."'

He finally dropped the Sinatra gags after being beaten up by a hoodlum wearing knuckledusters.

It is widely believed that author Mario Puzo based his Johnny Fontane character in *The Godfather* on Sinatra. In the film, the singer asks the Godfather for help in landing a film role, and when a producer initially refuses to cast Fontane he wakes up to find a decapitated horse's head alongside him in bed.

When Sinatra and Puzo came face to face in Las Vegas, Frank

let loose with a volley of abuse. 'He called me a pimp,' said Puzo. 'This rather flattered me. What hurt most of all was that here was a northern Italian threatening *me*, a southern Italian, with physical violence!'

Sinatra was never able to shake off his reputation for having connections with the Mafia. The FBI filed 1,275 pages on the subject, and it was the reason why President Kennedy eventually distanced himself from Sinatra after they had developed a close friendship.

Only Don Rickles could have got away with this gag: 'If one more person makes wrongful and slanderous accusations that Frank Sinatra has close links with the Mafia he will find himself sleeping with the fishes.'

Sometimes Sinatra's drunken tantrums left him the loser. He was once reported to have scalded a Las Vegas casino manager by tossing a cup of coffee over him. The manager, who was a heavyweight with huge shoulders, reacted by punching Sinatra so hard in the face that he removed his two front teeth. Old Blue Eyes (or should that be Black Eyes?) flew his personal dentist down to Vegas within twenty-four hours to insert a new pair of teeth at a cost of thousands of dollars.

But, of course, he had plenty of money for such indulgences. He once set up a helipad at his Los Angeles home solely to accommodate a presidential visit from his old drinking partner John F. Kennedy. But at the last minute JFK elected to stay with Bing Crosby instead. Sinatra was in such a rage ('Crosby is a f****** Republican,' he yelled) that he started to smash up the helipad with a sledgehammer.

He held JFK's brother-in-law Peter Lawford responsible for the President's change of plan, so he took the actor's suits from the guest-room wardrobe where he had left them during a previous visit and threw them into the swimming pool. Lawford was also kicked off the film *Robin and the Seven Hoods* . . . to be replaced, ironically, by Crosby. Although he went by the nickname 'Fixer', Lawford was never able to repair his relationship with the leader of the Pack.

So often the forgotten Rat Pack member, Lawford was a fascinating and ultimately very sad character. He was the handsome, debonair English-born son of Lady and Sir Sydney Lawford, and went to the States to start a film career in 1938. He gained entry into the Irish 'first family' of America when he married Patricia Kennedy in 1954, several years before her brother John made it to the White House.

With such good connections, he was like a magnet for Sinatra, who invited him into the exclusive Rat Pack club. It was through Lawford (or 'Brother-in-Lawford', as he was known to the rest of the Pack) that Sinatra first became close to JFK, and through him that the future President became even closer to screen goddess Marilyn Monroe.

Women found him irresistible. Of all the Rat Pack members,

Frank Sinatra (right) takes a drink as Dean Martin no doubt complains to Sammy Davis Jnr that he's hit a dry spell in one of the last Rat Pack performances.

he had the most notches on the bedroom post. His conquests (a veritable *Who's Who* of Hollywood crumpet in the 1950s and 1960s) reportedly included Ava Gardner, June Allyson, Lana Turner, Janet Leigh, Rita Hayworth, Dorothy Dandridge, Lucille Ball, Anne Baxter, Judy Holliday, Gina Lollobrigida, Judy Garland, Grace Kelly, Kim Novak, Jacqueline Kennedy Onassis, Lee Remick, Nancy Reagan, Elizabeth Taylor and Marilyn Monroe.

Soon after Sinatra turned his back on him, his wife divorced him (not surprisingly) on the grounds of his infidelity. His film work then dried up completely and he was reduced to accepting guest spots on television panel and quiz shows.

As a result of this depressing fall from stardom he became a hopeless alcoholic and spent much of his later life in the Betty Ford Clinic, before dying in 1984 at the age of sixty-one. His mother made no secret of what she thought of the way he had been treated: 'I don't know why Peter ever associated himself with that Rat Pack crowd,' she said. 'That dried-up piece of spaghetti – Sinatra – has been most disloyal. I do like his singing, but he's the villain of the piece.'

Doobie, doobie, doo.

Bing Crosby (Sinatra's idol when he was starting out) was an honorary member of the Rat Pack. In his youth, he would have been able to out-drink most of them, including Sinatra. Crosby was an alcoholic in the late 1920s, and his film career almost didn't take off because of the bad publicity he received for a drink-driving offence.

'Yes, I was very partial to the old hooch,' he admitted in later life. 'In my early days with the Rhythm Boys we liked our liquor so much that sometimes it took control. Often we three Rhythm Boys looked to me more like six. But when I see what Frank, Dean, Sammy and the fellers get through I think maybe I was an amateur.'

A new breed of Rat Packers – the Brat Pack – started hitting the booze-news headlines in the 1980s. They included Demi Moore (in a sort of Lauren Bacall role), Molly Ringwald (who could be seen as a latter-day Shirley MacLaine) and the hell-raising sons of actor Martin Sheen – Charlie Sheen and Emilio Estevez, the unofficial leader of the new pack.

Anthony Michael Hall, who specialised in playing nerds on the screen while drinking a quart of vodka every day off screen, set the pace. He admitted to being on this dangerous drink diet before he was seventeen. Bloody hell, I was not even on shandies at that age!

Fuelled by the liquor, he got involved in a series of drunken sprees and punch-ups, and admitted in a 1988 interview: 'A lot of performers get messed up because they think they don't deserve their success, but for me it was the opposite.'

Estevez, unlike his father and brother, proudly used his original Spanish family name. He featured in all of the key Brat Pack films – *The Outsiders* (1983), *The Breakfast Club* (1985) and *St Elmo's Fire* (1985) – and hung out at LA's Hard Rock Café, where he endlessly partied with fellow-eighties teen stars Rob Lowe, Tom Cruise and Sean Penn. He was also engaged to Demi Moore before she hooked up with Bruce Willis.

After his wild days, he later rejected the Brat Pack label, saying, 'We were just guys being guys. We'd meet to let off a little steam, that was all. We all have to grow up.'

He has since developed into a screenwriter of note, and he wrote, directed and starred in the hugely successful 2006 film *Bobby*, based on the last days of Robert Kennedy.

Never as out of control as his brother Charlie, he still recognises how drink can be a crutch. 'Writing is a lonely job,' he says, 'unless you're a drinker, in which case you always have a friend within reach.'

Rob Lowe was more in the mould of the Rat Pack pioneers, with the pursuit of women right up there in importance with the next drink. While partying with best buddies Estevez and Judd Nelson, he found the time to date a procession of beautiful, famous women, from actresses Melissa Gilbert ('I was a Brat Pack wife,' she claims) and Nastassja Kinski to Grace Jones, Brooke Shields and even Princess Stephanie of Monaco.

Before settling down to marriage with make-up artist Sheryl Berkoff, he said: 'If I haven't been with 'em, I know 'em, or I've been engaged to 'em. I looked at my calendar and said, "Shit, it's a few weeks into the New Year and I haven't been engaged to anyone yet. I'd better get to work."'

Now that's real Rat Pack talk!

Mel Gibson would also have slipped comfortably into the shoes – or on to the bar stool – of the Rat Packers. He has fallen off the wagon more times than is good for him, and got himself in a right old pickle when he was totally pickled in the summer of 2006.

After getting pulled over for speeding on the Pacific Coast Highway in Malibu, Gibson responded with an expletive-and-threat-filled tirade against the officer arresting him on suspicion of drink-driving. His outburst included anti-Semitic remarks and he tried to make a run (or a stagger) for it.

When he had sobered up, he issued the following contrite statement:

After drinking alcohol on Thursday night, I did a number of things that were very wrong and for which I am ashamed. I drove a car when I should not have, and was stopped by the LA County Sheriffs. The arresting officer was just doing his job and I feel fortunate that I was apprehended before I caused injury to any other person. I acted like a person completely out of control when I was arrested, and said things that I do not believe to be true and which are despicable. I am deeply ashamed of everything I said. Also, I take this opportunity to apologise to the deputies involved for my belligerent behaviour. They have always been there for me in my community and indeed probably saved me from myself. I disgraced myself and my family with my behaviour and for that I am truly sorry. I have battled with the disease of alcoholism for all of my adult life and profoundly regret my horrific relapse. I apologise for any behaviour unbecoming of me in my inebriated state and have already taken necessary steps to ensure my return to health.

Mournful Mel was found guilty and instructed to seek help in rehab.

There was less mercy for hotel heiress Paris Hilton when she broke a motoring probation ruling after being arrested for reckless driving while over the limit.

Paris – one of the new, irritating breed of socialites who are famous merely for being famous – was given a forty-five-day jail sentence. So she went from drinking bars to behind bars. We can only hope there was no room service for her while she was inside.

In the end, she served just twenty-four days, but on her release she talked about her ordeal as if she had been locked away for years. She might have the same sort of financial clout as the Rat Pack, but she doesn't have any of their class.

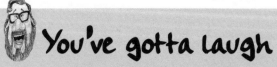

You've gotta laugh

Mrs Kathleen O'Toole was at home making dinner as usual when her husband's best friend Seamus Finnegan knocked at her door.

'Kathleen, may I come in?' he asks. 'I've got some bad news, I'm afraid.'

She has a sudden dread and sits down. 'Nothing's happened to my husband Tommy, has it?'

'That's what I'm here to tell you, Kath. There was an accident down at the Guinness brewery.'

'Oh God, no!' cries Kathleen. 'Please don't tell me . . .'

'I must, Kathleen. Tommy is dead and gone. I'm sorry.'

Kathleen weeps uncontrollably, then pulls herself together enough to ask how it happened.

'It was terrible, Kathleen, so it was. He fell head first into a vat of Guinness and drowned.'

'Oh, my dear Jesus!' says Kathleen. 'Please tell me he didn't suffer. Was it at least quick?'

'Well, not really, Kathleen. Fact is, he got out three times to piss.'

Hark Who's Talking About Drink

'I've been on an alcoholic diet, and have lost three days already.'
– Tommy Cooper

'An alcoholic is someone you don't like who drinks as much as you do.'
– Dylan Thomas

'My dad was the town drunk. Most of the time that's not so bad; but New York City?'
– Henry Youngman

'I don't like people who take drugs . . . customs officers, for instance.'
– Mike Reid

'Prohibition is better than no liquor at all.'
– Will Rogers

'I once shook hands with Pat Boone and my whole right side suddenly sobered up.'
– Dean Martin

'I am certainly not a heavy drinker. Why, I can sometimes go hours without a drop passing my lips.'
– Noël Coward

'The beer was so weak it couldn't get out of the glass.'
– Max Miller

'What thinks you make I am drunk, Officer?'
– Ted Rogers

'Alcohol is not addictive. I should know. I've been drinking for years.'
– Tallulah Bankhead

'Giving up drinking is easy. I've done it hundreds of times.'
– Spike Milligan

'One day recently a man called out to me from the other side of the street asking me for the price of a drink. I beckoned him to come over for it and he waved me away. This has to be the Everest of laziness.'
– Jeffrey Bernard

'The biggest loser I know is the man who went into hospital for a liver transplant and got Oliver Reed's.'
– John Edwards

'I was advised to drink a hair of the dog to cure my hangover. Now I've got distemper.'
– Les Dawson

'I make it a rule never to drink while I'm sleeping.'
– Dickie Henderson

5 Flash, Bang, Wallop!

A new phenomenon has entered the often-crazy world of show-business – stand-up, fall-down fights between pissed-off and frequently pissed-up celebrities and the paparazzi.

When you are in the public eye, I promise the paparazzi can be pests. And it's not only the professionals that you need to worry about. Everyone with a camera now seems to fancy himself as David Bailey, and they snatch pictures of celebrities without as much as a by-your-leave.

When you come out of, say, an awards ceremony, often nicely warmed by the hospitality booze, the last thing you want is somebody sticking a camera in your face; particularly when you've got a mug as ugly as mine! All right, I'll admit they don't exactly flock after me, but I have witnessed many of my more photogenic colleagues having their lives ruined by the paps. You might be fair game when you're at some public event, but those photographers who get out the long lenses to snatch pictures of people in private moments are lower than peeping toms in my opinion. They should be told where to stick their tripods!

Admittedly, a lot of the photographers act with dignity and respectfully ask permission before clicking away, but there is a growing army of camera mercenaries who take not only pictures but liberties.

As I suppose you already know, the word 'paparazzi' comes

from the 1960 Federico Fellini film *La Dolce Vita*. One of the main characters – portrayed by Walter Santesso – is a photographer called Paparazzo. He was based on a boy Fellini knew at school who was always buzzing around, full of energy and non-stop chatter. *Paparazzo* in Italian means mosquito, but the paparazzi making nuisances of themselves nowadays with celebrities (and often making fortunes with their photographs) are more like vultures than mosquitoes.

Just to give an idea of how much money a specialist paparazzo can make, Los Angeles-based photographer Mel Bouzard revealed that he had scooped more than $150,000 for just one snatched picture of Ben Affleck and Jennifer Lopez following their break-up. And the rates have shot up since then: a similar picture now could rake in over a million dollars!

What we should be asking, I suppose, is whether the paparazzi are the problem or if they are just feeding the cravings of what has become a voyeuristic society. You only have to see the sales figures of 'celebrity' magazines to realise that the general public cannot get enough of peering into the private lives of the stars.

In this chapter, I will be providing a few examples of where it has all got out of hand. I freely admit that, in most cases, my sympathy lies with the personality being photographed rather than with the uninvited, uncouth paparazzi pests. Alcohol is not always involved in these stories, but let me assure you that what some photographers get up to can drive you to drink!

The two young royal princes are top of the fee league for snatched photographs, regardless of the fact that their mother, Princess Diana, was continually plagued by the paparazzi right up to her death in the car crash in Paris.

Prince Harry seems to find the intrusion hard to handle, and he has often been photographed losing his temper as the paps close in on him.

A glass in hand and a blonde to be kissed . . . Prince Harry is a goldmine for the paparazzi.

He made worldwide front-page news when tangling with a photographer outside Boujis nightclub in London, where it was alleged he had spent the evening downing 'Crack Baby' cocktails. Nirach Tanner, a freelance photographer, told reporters: 'He screamed at me to f*** off, then grabbed me by the collar and tried to shove me over.'

I would have been at Harry's side helping him. I'm not advocating that he should be out on the piss, but he has the same right as everybody else to get hammered without the world and his wife knowing all about it.

Mounting tensions between the paparazzi and their prey reached fever pitch in the spring of 2007 when it emerged that Hugh Grant had been arrested for allegedly assaulting a photographer. It became known as the 'Great Battle of the Tin of Beans'.

The paps were out in force close to Grant's Chelsea home, where it was alleged that Hugh, in a fury, threw the aforementioned projectile at snapper Ian Whittaker. The photographer claimed he had been left 'bruised, battered and covered in baked beans'. It was obviously a serious affair for Grant and Whittaker, but the rest of us found it hilarious, and many applauded Grant for his stand (not to mention his aim).

It was the latest high-profile conflict between a celebrity and those who earn their living capturing their every move, and it was further evidence that the famous are fighting back against the unwanted intrusion of the camera lens.

Newspapers published pictures of the alleged assault by Grant, appearing to show him kicking and kneeing the photographer in the groin. Whittaker claimed that the actor swore at him and lashed out after he was asked to smile for the camera. He also asserted that Grant said of the photographer's two children: 'I hope they die of f****** cancer.'

Grant strenuously denied the final allegation.

It all then became the business of the legal eagles, which means I can make no further comment, other than to say that the throwing of the can of beans was a masterstroke by a man who wants to have the paparazzi on toast.

Hugh should consider forming a tag team with Brad Pitt as his partner. In 2005, following his split with Jennifer Aniston, the American heart-throb reportedly pelted intrusive photographers with a fusillade of eggs. They just need to find a celebrity whose weapon of choice is rashers of bacon and they'll be able to give the paparazzi a breakfast to remember!

Of course, by fighting back, these celebs are playing right into the hands of the paparazzi. The mob will willingly sacrifice one of their number to get pictures of a well-known person losing control.

Popstrel Lily Allen recently aimed a kung-fu kick at a female photographer and tried to wrestle her camera from her. Lily had been drinking in London's Groucho Club until the early hours, and it was on her exit that the fracas flared up. Her boyfriend, Seb Chew, stepped in to calm things down, but later a stoked-up Lily – daughter of the equally boisterous actor Keith Allen – reportedly lashed out at another photographer before she was ushered away by her companions.

It might have been better for Lily if she had taken her own advice and smiled instead.

Jay Kay, the lead singer with Jamiroquai, has had plenty of headline-hitting run-ins with the paparazzi. He was arrested and cautioned in September 2006 for attacking a photographer outside Soho's Kabaret Club. It was like an action replay for Kay, who had suffered a bloodied nose following an altercation after a film premiere in 2002. The year before that, he was accused of attacking a member of the paparazzi and smashing his equipment outside a London nightclub. The charges were dropped due to lack of evidence.

One of the photographers allegedly punched by Kay – as he came out of a nightclub obviously the worse for wear – said: 'He called me a gay boy from the south and then took a swing at me. For some reason he thought we were trying to take pictures of him, when we were only there because of a tip-off that Lindsay Lohan was in the club. Jay Kay was out of his head, and we had no interest in him whatsoever. Perhaps that's why he whacked me.'

The interest in *Mean Girls* actress Lohan exploded after she fell out with film bosses during the shooting of *Georgia Rule* in 2006. Taking a break from filming, Lindsay and several companions allegedly arrived intoxicated at an after-hours gathering at Disneyland. It was reported that there was fighting and brawling among the guests. (Goodness knows what Mickey and Pluto made of it!) The promotional visit was cut short by theme park officials, who claimed the group's behaviour was offensive and abusive.

It got worse when the chief executive of the company making *Georgia Rule* sent a red-hot warning letter to Lindsay, which was soon leaked to the press:

Since the commencement of principal photography of Georgia Rule, *you have frequently failed to arrive on time to the set. Today, you did not show for work. I am now told you don't plan to work tomorrow because you are 'not feeling well'. You and your representatives have told us that your various late arrivals and absences from the set have been the result of illness; today we were told it was 'heat exhaustion'. We are well aware that your ongoing all night heavy partying is the real reason for your so called 'exhaustion'. We refuse to accept bogus excuses for your behavior.*

To date, your actions on Georgia Rule *have been discourteous, irresponsible and unprofessional. You have acted like a spoiled child and in so doing have alienated many of your coworkers and endangered the quality of this picture. Moreover, your actions have resulted in hundreds of thousands of dollars in damage. We will not tolerate these actions any further.*

If you do not honor your production commitments, including your scheduled call time for tomorrow, and any call times thereafter, we will hold you personally accountable. This means that in addition to pursuing full monetary damages, we will take such other action as we deem necessary to preserve the integrity of the Georgia Rule *production as well as [our] financial interests. I urge you to take this letter seriously and conduct yourself professionally.*

Ouch! I doubt any of the Hollywood hell-raisers from the Errol Flynn/Clark Gable/Humphrey Bogart era ever got a letter like that from their studio bosses. And Lindsay was just twenty years old at the time.

The letter worked. Lohan woke up to her responsibilities, finished the film (giving a stunning performance as, *natch*, a rebellious, uncontrollable teenager) and even kissed and made up with the studio bosses.

However, in the summer of 2007 she was in trouble again after a car crash, with drink and drugs pushing her back into the headlines. This time she needed more than a warning letter, and wisely booked in for rehab treatment.

Mixed-up singer Britney Spears has had more run-ins with the paparazzi than I've had hot curries. One widely circulated picture showed her attacking a photographer's car with an umbrella outside her home in Los Angeles, shortly after separating from her husband, Kevin Federline.

Britney claimed in a 2006 interview that the microscopic scrutiny from the paps had made her an 'emotional wreck', and she pleaded: 'I need privacy and I need respect; they are things you have to have as human beings.'

That made good sense to me, even though it was countered by claims from photographers that they often got tip-offs from Britney herself when she was going to make an appearance.

A lot of stars feed off the publicity they get from the paparazzi, so I suppose those who try to manipulate the machine cannot pick and choose when the photographers shadow them.

What is it with the young stars today? Do they struggle to hold their drink? You never caught Shirley Temple coming out of a nightclub as pissed as a newt. (Although, come to think of it, I'm not so sure you could say the same about Judy Garland!)

As we saw in the previous chapter, Paris Hilton draws the paparazzi like bees to a honey-pot, and she rarely fails to give them something to make them click.

The heiress and glamorous actress Bijou Phillips were caught up in a fight outside Los Angeles hotspot Mood in 2005. They looked more than merry when leaving the club after partying with Bruce Willis, Eddie Murphy and Lindsay Lohan. Then all hell broke loose when Hilton's bodyguard flattened a photographer who got too close. His fellow-snappers were torn between joining in the fight or taking what were potentially lucrative pictures of the mayhem.

After being shepherded to her silver Bentley, Paris calmly sat signing more dignified photographs of herself.

Photographers needed to be either brave or stupid to ignore demands from Mike Tyson to stop snapping him in a São Paulo nightclub where drink was flowing in 2005.

Most of the paparazzi retreated under threat from the ex-world heavyweight champion, who used to be known as 'the most dangerous man on the planet'.

But one TV cameraman decided that fortune favours the brave. He was wrong! As he went for one more shot Tyson leapt at him, snatched his camera, pulled out and destroyed the videotape, and then – according to witnesses – thumped the cameraman. It generated 'Tyson Goes Nuts in Brazil' headlines.

Crash, bang, wallop . . . what a picture!

Gladiator star Russell Crowe could challenge Tyson as to which heavyweight strikes most fear into the paparazzi. He has had a long-running battle with the street photographers who try to record his every move, often when he has been out on the town.

But his punch-ups are not always drink-fuelled. He was perfectly sober when he threatened to 'tar and feather' any photographer who as much as pointed a camera at his wife Dani, who at the time was heavily pregnant with their second child. It is easy to understand his reaction when you hear what happened with their first baby.

'Dani was three weeks early last time,' explained Crowe. 'She gave birth just a few days after she was chased down the street by four photographers. She was just walking down the street with her girlfriend and they rushed her – four of them surrounded her. So she panicked and slipped . . . If I'd been there that would have been a really serious situation.'

Sean Penn gained a reputation for being the most consistent puncher of paparazzi in his wild young days, particularly when he was married to Madonna and saw it as his duty to protect her from the prying

Sean Penn went to extreme lengths to protect his then wife Madonna from the paparazzi during the 1980s.

cameras. He was also known to shoot at helicopters from which photographers were trying to snatch pictures, and wrote a huge message to them in the sand: 'F*** OFF' (only he didn't use asterisks!).

According to the Penn legend, his most frightening act of retribution – after finding a photographer hiding in his ninth-floor hotel room in Macau – was to hold him by his ankles over the balcony!

In 1987, ex-boxer Penn served thirty-four days in jail for punching an extra on the set of *Colors* who was trying to take his picture.

He now admits that many of his early off-set dramas with the paparazzi were drink-fuelled: 'Let's say I spent some time investigating the adventures of alcohol like a lot of young American boys,' he recalls.

He has a permanent reminder of his drunken escapades: a scar over his right eyebrow that is a memento of a bar fight.

Following Princess Diana's death while being chased by paparazzi, Penn made it clear that he thought his aggressive attitude had been vindicated. The Screen Actors Guild subsequently invited him to appear on a panel investigating privacy and the press. 'I'm not out there like some kind of madman,' Penn said, 'but just try having somebody follow you around all the time. When somebody with a prettier face than mine gets killed in a tunnel then it's, ooh, we have to do something. But, bottom line, the paparazzi's abusive freedom of the press will be protected more enduringly than the individual's.'

Scottish actor Ewan McGregor was even more outspoken in a vicious attack on *Heat*, one of the celebrity magazines that has featured snatched pictures of him. 'That magazine is a dirty, filthy piece of sh*t and I'd like to put that on record,' he told the *Guardian*. 'People shouldn't buy it because it sucks. If a guy comes up and asks me, "Can I take a picture of your daughter?" that's one thing. But if he's hiding behind a bus and he takes a picture of me and my daughter he's legally allowed to publish that photo in the press. I have no rights to stop him and I think that's wrong. I think we should encourage people to beat up paparazzi.'

McGregor did not resort to violence himself, but he hit the paparazzi where it *really* hurts by winning an invasion of privacy case against a leading photographer. The action related to photographs taken of the McGregor children while they were on holiday with their father in Mauritius. As part of the settlement, the defendants agreed to pay damages and costs, and gave undertakings not to take further pictures of the children.

Actress Reese Witherspoon also went down the legal road against photographers, whom she claimed had consistently trapped her in public places and hurled abuse at her in a bid to get her to react angrily.

'They've hit my car and tried to push me off the road,' she said, 'and they've blocked me in with their cars, which is false imprisonment. They shout terrible obscene things at me and my children to try and get a reaction. I had one follow us to the paediatrician's office shouting the f-word at us. My daughter was only four – she was shaking and crying.

'It's hard to live with. And I don't understand why it's legal to print pictures of my children.'

Reese lost the case, but took hope from a piece of legislation pushed through the California State Congress by a man who knows all about pressure from the paparazzi – Governor Arnold Schwarzenegger.

Photographers had once run The Governator and his family off the road during a car chase, but he exacted revenge by introducing the new law which restricted 'hardcore' photographers from harming the public. Anyone who commits assault in an attempt to get a photograph or video recording is now liable to pay triple damages and give up any profits made from the illegally taken picture or film.

The granddaddy of the paparazzi was the American Ron Galella, who became a legend in the industry even before the term was coined. His technique of catching his subjects in everyday settings or surprising them to capture their reactions was hugely innovative in the 1950s.

In 1972 he lodged a complaint against Jackie Kennedy Onassis and three Secret Service agents for alleged false arrest, malicious prosecution and interference with trade. Onassis vigorously fought the complaint, citing in court that Galella had taken pictures of her son John Kennedy Jnr when he was riding his bicycle in Central Park. She claimed that the photographer had jumped into the boy's path, causing the three agents to spring into action themselves. They arrested and interrogated Galella, but released him when they realised he was not a potential kidnapper.

It was also pointed out in court that Galella had previously interrupted Jackie's daughter Caroline while she was playing tennis, and had invaded both children's private schools. On another occasion he had come uncomfortably close in a powerboat to Jackie herself while she was swimming.

Onassis testified that Galella often 'jumped and postured around' while taking pictures of her. It was claimed that he habitually bribed apartment, restaurant and nightclub doormen and even romanced a family servant to keep him advised of the movements of the family.

Galella lost the case and was restricted from coming within a hundred yards of the Onassis home and fifty yards of Jackie or her children.

But his run-in with Jackie-O was only part of the Galella legend. He made such a pest of himself with Brigitte Bardot that she organised 'a posse' which soaked him with a hose. And after he attempted to take candid photos of Richard Burton and Elizabeth Taylor in Mexico, Burton's bodyguards kicked Galella in the jaw and roughed him up after discovering his hiding-place.

Sean Penn was less physical: he merely took to spitting at the veteran photographer.

But it was Marlon Brando who went to the greatest lengths to stop Galella photographing him in private moments. He himself attacked the paparazzo (Brando was always more of a genuine hard man than Burton) and left him with a broken jaw and four missing teeth!

Did Galella back off? What do you think? From then on, whenever he was tracking Brando, he simply wore an American football helmet for protection.

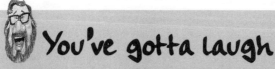

You've gotta laugh

An extremely shy, private man is sitting in the corner of a West End pub having a quiet drink when he catches the eye of a beautiful woman sitting at the bar. He blushes and looks away, before snatching another glance and sees that she is still looking at him. He is convinced she is giving him the come on, so after another courage-boosting drink he forces himself to go over.

He slips on to a stool alongside her at the bar. 'Uh . . . er . . . would you mind very much if I . . . uh . . . sat down and talked to you for a while?' he asks.

The woman looks at him as if he has just crawled out from under a stone and yells so loudly that everybody in the bar hears: 'No, I won't sleep with you. Are you f****** nuts?'

The whole bar falls silent and the man blushes as he becomes aware that everyone is staring at him. He wishes the floor would swallow him up as he returns to his corner seat.

A few minutes later, the woman walks over and apologises. Smiling at him, she says: 'I'm sorry for embarrassing you, but I'm a psychology student studying how people respond to suddenly unexpected situations.'

The mouse suddenly becomes a man. 'What?' he yells loudly. 'Two hundred quid? You *must* be f****** joking.'

Hark Who's Talking About Drink

'This is one of the disadvantages of wine: it makes a man mistake words for thought.'
– Samuel Johnson

'What's drinking? A mere pause from thinking.'
– Lord Byron

'Without question, the greatest invention in the history of mankind is beer. Oh, I grant you that the wheel was also a fine invention, but the wheel does not go nearly as well with pizza.'
– Dave Barry

'Drinking makes such fools of people, and people are such fools to begin with, that it's compounding a felony.'
– Robert Benchley

'Champagne, if you are seeking the truth, is better than a lie detector. It encourages a man to be expansive, even reckless, while lie detectors are only a challenge to tell lies successfully.'
– Graham Greene

'I'll stick with gin. Champagne is just ginger ale that knows somebody.'
– Alan Alda

'Even though a number of people have tried, no one has yet found a way to drink for a living.'
– Jean Kerr

'Uncork the bottle to uncork your wit.'
– John Edwards

'Drunkenness is temporary suicide.'
– Bertrand Russell

'If we take habitual drunkards as a class, their heads and their hearts will bear an advantageous comparison with those of any other class. There seems ever to have been a proneness in the brilliant and warm-blooded to fall in to this vice. The demon of intemperance ever seems to have delighted in sucking the blood of genius and generosity.'
– Abraham Lincoln

'Good health . . . that's what my friends are always drinking to before they fall down.'
– Phyllis Diller

'The waiter tried to charge me for vintage wine. I said that I was not falling for that old one.'
– Jimmy Wheeler

'I find it much more fun to be a little drunk than a lot sober.'
- Robert Morley

'One Martini is all right. Two are too many, and three are not enough.'
- James Thurber

6 **The Great Pub Quiz**

As we approach the halfway house, let's get right into pub mode. Everybody's doing it, from university dons to road-sweepers, football idols to idle pharmacists, housewives to horse-whisperers. They are all taking part in pub quizzes: it is estimated that more than two million people in the UK participate in them at least once a week. I know some folk from Liverpool who make a living out of it, travelling up and down the country to compete for prize money armed with heads full of trivia.

To help you recreate the excitement of the pub quiz in your own home, my know-all writing partner Norman Giller and I have come up with our own thirty-question quiz. We give multiple-choice options, including the correct answer, some red herrings and an occasional silly choice. You must get at least sixteen right to pass our test. Then try it on your friends, and see if they can beat your score. We give the answers at the end of the chapter.

So, if you're sitting comfortably, here we go with the *Cheers My Arse* Pub Quiz . . .

1. Who was the first author to write a novel on a typewriter?
a) Charles Dickens
b) Mark Twain
c) H.G. Wells
d) William Shakespeare

2. Which one of these entertainers did not wear a hairpiece?

a) Frank Sinatra

b) Gene Kelly

c) Dean Martin

d) Bing Crosby

3. Which city has the most Rolls-Royces per person?

a) London

b) Hong Kong

c) Gotham

d) New York

4. Which family lives at 742 Evergreen Terrace?

a) The Bushes

b) The Addamses

c) The Krays

d) The Simpsons

5. Which country has won the Eurovision Song Contest most times?

a) Spain

b) France

c) Chile

d) Ireland

6. Yul Brynner played The King, but who was 'I' in the film version of The King and I?

a) Deborah Kerr

b) Doris Day

c) Rita Hayworth

d) Britney Spears

7. In The Flintstones what is the name of Fred and Wilma's daughter?

a) Pebbles

b) Marbles
c) Jagger
d) Sandy

8. Bill Pratt was the real name of which film star?
a) Fred Astaire
b) Marlon Brando
c) William Holden
d) Boris Karloff

9. Which American city is named after a British Prime Minister?
a) Charleston
b) Washington
c) Cleveland
d) Pittsburgh

10. Which one of these did not have a glass eye?
a) Peter Falk
b) Orson Welles
c) Leo McKern
d) Rex Harrison

11. Who was not born in Scotland?
a) Sean Connery
b) Ewan McGregor
c) Tony Blair
d) Rod Stewart

12. Which of these film stars did not marry eight times?
a) Elizabeth Taylor
b) Lana Turner
c) Mickey Rooney
d) Stan Laurel

13. What was discovered in a flat in the very first scene of the BBC soap EastEnders?
a) Stolen banknotes
b) A dying man
c) Barbara Windsor's wig
d) An escaped prisoner

14. Which one of these cricketers was born in England?
a) Ted Dexter
b) Bob Woolmer
c) Colin Cowdrey
d) Len Hutton

15. Who was a bank clerk before switching to a broadcasting career?
a) Terry Wogan
b) Jonathan Ross
c) Trevor McDonald
d) Jimmy Savile

16. Whose name appears at the end of every episode of Coronation Street as the theme composer?
a) Tony Hatch
b) Roger Daltrey
c) Eric Spear
d) Edward Elgar

17. In which seaside resort was Fawlty Towers set?
a) Brighton
b) Margate
c) Monte Carlo
d) Torquay

18. Who won the Eurovision Song Contest with 'Puppet on a String'?
a) Sandie Shaw
b) Bucks Fizz
c) Lulu
d) Andy Pandy

19. Which one of these legends lived beyond the age of 25?
a) James Dean
b) Buddy Holly
c) Billy the Kid
d) Jimi Hendrix

20. Who has the middle name Hercules?
a) Elton John
b) Ozzy Osbourne
c) Bob Dylan
d) Alice Cooper

21. Which US President saw active service in both the First and the Second World Wars?
a) Harry Truman
b) Richard Nixon
c) Lyndon Johnson
d) Dwight Eisenhower

22. In which town was the gunfight at the OK Corral?
a) Dallas, Texas
b) Tombstone, Arizona
c) Miami, Florida
d) Dodge City, Kansas

23. Which post-war FA Cup-winning team cost just £110 in signing-on fees?
a) Chelsea
b) Aston Villa
c) Bolton Wanderers
d) Charlton Athletic

24. What's the main alcoholic ingredient of a Bloody Mary?
a) Gin
b) Vodka
c) Rum
d) Guinness

25. Where would you find the Canal Turn?
a) Silverstone
b) Brands Hatch
c) Ascot
d) Aintree

26. Who used to play piano in a French brothel?
a) André Previn
b) Russ Conway
c) Les Dawson
d) Dudley Moore

27. What did Julius Caesar, Napoleon Bonaparte and Benito Mussolini have in common?
a) A fear of confined spaces
b) A fear of snakes
c) A fear of blood
d) A fear of cats

28. What was the last port of call of the Titanic?
a) Cork
b) Liverpool

c) Southampton

d) Calais

29. Which country has most universities?

a) Russia

b) China

c) India

d) United States

30. Who was the Scouse comedian who hosted the TV quiz show Winner Takes All?

a) Jimmy Tarbuck

b) Les Dennis

c) Ken Dodd

d) Stan Boardman

ANSWERS:

1. b) Mark Twain (*Tom Sawyer*)

2. c) Dean Martin

3. b) Hong Kong

4. d) The Simpsons

5. d) Ireland (seven times)

6. a) Deborah Kerr

7. a) Pebbles

8. d) Boris Karloff

9. d) Pittsburgh (William Pitt)

10. b) Orson Welles

11. d) Rod Stewart (born in Highgate, London)

12. b) Lana Turner (married 'only' seven times)

13. b) A dying man

14. d) Len Hutton

15. a) Terry Wogan

16. c) Eric Spear

17. d) Torquay
18. a) Sandie Shaw
19. d) Jimi Hendrix (died aged twenty-seven)
20. a) Elton John
21. d) Dwight Eisenhower
22. b) Tombstone, Arizona
23. c) Bolton Wanderers (1958)
24. b) Vodka
25. d) Aintree
26. c) Les Dawson
27. d) A fear of cats
28. a) Cork
29. c) India (with more than seven thousand)
30. a) Jimmy Tarbuck

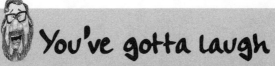

You've gotta laugh

A man sitting alone at the bar thinks he is hearing things. 'Ooooh, you are fantastic,' a voice says. 'Definitely the best-dressed, most handsome man in the pub.' The man looks around and then realises that the voice is coming from the bowl of peanuts in front of him.

Suddenly there is an interruption from the direction of the fruit machine. 'You're talking rubbish,' the new voice says. 'Look at the state of his shoes, and his hair is a mess.'

The man is beginning to wonder if he has drunk too much when the barman tells him: 'I'm sorry, sir. The nuts are complimentary, but the fruit machine is out of order.'

Hark Who's Being Insulting About Drink

'It's not the drinking that's Deano's problem. It's the drinking between the drinking.'
- Frank Sinatra

'The last time Jack Benny bought a drink it was poured by a Roman slave.'
- Bob Hope

'Was he drunk? He was as legless as Douglas Bader.'
- Golfer Max Faulkner, describing his drunken caddie

'The beer was so warm that I used it in my hot-water bottle.'
- Danny Kaye, unable to find a cold beer at his London hotel

'Landlord, I have enjoyed drinking in many great saloons – but this isn't one of them.'
- Groucho Marx

'The bartender did not have a clue how to mix a Martini. I think he got his training on a cement mixer.'
- David Niven

'The barmaid served such short measures that we nicknamed her Milly Metre.'
- John Edwards

'They've stopped us smoking in pubs. Next they'll stop us farting. And then they'll stop us drinking.'
- Johnny Vegas

'I told the bartender that he'd put more ice in my whisky than there'd been in the berg that sank the *Titanic*.'
- W.C. Fields

'I love the quaintness of English pubs. Pity about the beer. No wonder we demanded our independence!'
- Bing Crosby

'The landlord was such a miserable git that even his beer scowled at you.'
- Warren Mitchell

'Two sisters came into the pub and I asked if they had left Cinderella at home. Suddenly I was wearing my drink.'
- Ted Rogers

7 Hollywood's Legless Legends

Master director Alfred Hitchcock once said: 'You can take a horse to water, but you can't force it to drink . . . just as sure as you can take an actor to Hollywood, and you can't stop him drinking.'

There is something about the magnetism of Hollywood that draws many stars into a drinking culture that eventually wrecks their lives. So the consolation for me in not having cracked Hollywood is that I avoided the alcoholic minefield . . . or perhaps that should be the alcoholic lake.

Imagine Jim Royle let loose in LA! Having served and survived his apprenticeship at The Feathers he would have drunk Hollywood dry. City of Angels My Arse!

In the interests of medical science (all right, in the interests of your entertainment), I have tried to discover who have been the most legless Hollywood legends. But before the lawyers start licking their lips, I have to tell them that I confined my search to those screen stars who are now plying their trade on the great film set in the sky. So modern hell-raisers like Charlie Sheen, Warren Beatty, Robert Downey Jnr, Dennis Hopper, Mickey Rourke, Russell Crowe, Sean Penn, Nick Nolte, Johnny Depp and Mel Gibson have avoided close scrutiny . . . in this chapter at least.

The method of picking the top ten Hollywood drunks was hardly scientific, but plenty of column inches in fading news-papers and drink-related mentions on the internet were totted up to give the kings (and one sad queen) of the Hollywood Bar-room of Fame. Here they are, in time-honoured reverse order:

10 Spencer Tracy For years the Hollywood studio publicity machine fought to hide the fact that Spencer Tracy had recurring alcoholic problems. He was considered by many good judges to have been America's finest actor (check out *Northwest Passage*, *Bad Day at Black Rock*, *Inherit the Wind*, *Father of the Bride* and *The Last Hurrah* to name but five of his classics). But what was little known outside the small world of Hollywood itself was that Tracy often got lost in an alcoholic haze between his movies.

Admitting late in his life that he had a problem, he said: 'I used to go on two-hour lunch breaks that lasted two weeks.' These were huge benders, and one of the few people who could help him through each crisis was his long-time closet lover Katharine Hepburn.

'Mr Tracy, you're not as tall as I expected,' she said when producer Joe Mankiewicz first introduced her to the man who was to become her partner on and off screen.

'Don't worry, Kate,' Mankiewicz interjected, 'he'll soon cut you down to size.'

They became inseparable, and for many years were the hottest double act in the film world, co-starring in nine films, including *Adam's Rib*, *Woman of the Year*, *Pat and Mike*, and their last film together, which was completed shortly before Tracy's death, *Guess Who's Coming to Dinner*.

By then, Hepburn had taken almost five years out of her own career to nurse Tracy through his last days when he was suffering from emphysema and alcohol-related problems. But it was never easy for her when he was really hitting the bottle. She recalled trying to get him to bed one night when he struck her with the back of his hand (for which he profusely apologised when he sobered up). 'But I never thought of leaving him,' she told her biographer. 'What would have been the point? I loved him and wanted to be with him. If I had left we would have both been miserable.'

He was almost equally adored by his male colleagues. Humphrey Bogart, who sank many a glass with Tracy (and is missing from this list only because he featured so prominently in the Rat Pack chapter), said: 'Spence is the best actor we have, because you don't see the mechanism at work. He makes it all look so natural and so easy.'

In a 1986 television documentary on Tracy, Hepburn shared with viewers a letter she had written to him eighteen years after his death as she pondered why he always seemed to seek escape in a bottle:

Living wasn't easy for you, was it? What did you like to do? Sailing – especially in stormy weather. You loved polo, but tennis, golf, swimming – no, not really. Walking – no, that didn't suit you – that was one of those things where you could think at the same time. Of this, of that . . . of what, Spence, what was it? Was it some specific thing, like being a Catholic and you felt a bad Catholic? You concentrated on all the bad, none of the good which your religion offered. It must've been something very fundamental, very ever present. And the incredible fact that there you were, really the greatest movie actor – you could do it, and you could do it with that glorious simplicity, that directness. You couldn't enter your own life, but you could be someone else. You were the character in a moment, you hardly had to study – what a relief, you could be someone else for a while, you weren't you, you were safe. And then back to life's trials: 'Oh, hell, take a drink. Yes. No. Maybe.' And then stop taking those drinks – you were great at that, Spence, you could just stop. How I respected you for that – very unusual. But why the escape hatch? Why was it always open? To get away from the remarkable you. I always meant to ask you. Did you know what it was? Are you having a long rest after all your tossing and turning in life? Are you happy finally?

Nobody will know the answers, but we do know that he left behind a treasure chest of films that prove he was one of the greatest actors that ever breathed.

9 Robert Mitchum Before anybody had defined the word, Robert Mitchum was 'cool'. There could be few from my generation (with a seat in the theatre of dreams for a couple of shillings) who did not imagine themselves in a Robert Mitchum pose, a late night tumbler of whiskey in hand, a pack of unfiltered cigarettes, a trench coat with the collar upturned, a fedora with the brim downturned, oozing strength and sexuality. I often wonder how I ended up as Jim Royle in my smelly sweater and baggy jeans.

Throughout his long career, the hooded-eyed Mitchum pretended to regard the acting profession casually, repeatedly

Robert Mitchum, the epitomy of cool and with a glass rarely far out of reach.

remarking in his drawling baritone, 'It sure as hell beats working.'

Yet he was widely respected in the film business as being a dedicated, no-nonsense craftsman who was always punctual, word perfect in his lines and continually looking for the flawless take. He appeared in war movies, Westerns and *films noirs*. He was equally convincing as a villain in old black-and-white Hopalong Cassidy movies, a heroic GI or a battle-weary officer, a flinty private eye (probably the best-ever Philip Marlowe) or a homicidal killer.

'I think when producers have a part that's hard to cast, they say, "Send for Mitchum; he'll do anything,"' he once remarked. 'I don't care what I play. I'll do Polish, psychos, gays, women, midgets, anything. Just don't forget to sign the cheque.'

Off screen, he could drink with the best of them, and his love for alcohol became such an issue that he was one of the first celebrities to book into the Betty Ford Clinic. But we should doff our hats (fedoras, of course) to Bob for never allowing his booze dependency to interfere with his work.

His life reads like something out of the sort of Hollywood movie to which he impressively used to lend his brooding presence. Born in Bridgeport, Connecticut, in 1917, he survived a close-to-poverty childhood. His Irish-descended railway-worker father was killed in an accident when he was just two, so he was brought up by his Norwegian mother. Leaving school at fourteen, he rode the rails with the hobos in the 'buddy can you spare a dime' Depression years and, in a yarn he loved to spin, escaped from a Georgia chain gang at fifteen to become one of Hollywood's most enduring stars.

He was literally a hungry fighter in his youth, having twenty-seven contests as a professional boxer, but decided a career change was called for after a defeat that left him with his nose spread across his face. When it was once suggested by a studio boss that he should have the injured hooter repaired, he said: 'It's already been fixed, by four left hooks.'

Mitchum thought he had blown his film career almost before

it had started when he was jailed for marijuana possession in 1948 after a raid on the home of a film starlet with whom he was having an intimate relationship.

He was sentenced to sixty days on a prison farm and made big headlines on his release when he declared: 'It's just like Palm Springs without the riff-raff.'

Rather than harming his career, though, the jail experience gave it a boost, and he was rarely out of work for the next forty years, making more than a hundred films, and always controlling his booze intake when he had a production schedule.

For years he was against 'that dangerous box in the corner', but he reversed his stand against television in the 1980s when appearing in *The Winds of War*. As Navy Captain Pug Henry, he won acclaim and awards for his hugely impressive performance.

Mitchum was flown secretly to London to collect one of his awards. It was all very hush-hush that he was to be the surprise last guest on a *TV Times* show, and there was even a news blackout to stop anybody finding out before the live programme.

He arrived too late for a rehearsal and was shown to the green room, where he proceeded to fill a huge pipe with what one onlooker described as 'the biggest wedge of weed I have ever seen'. Clearly, almost four decades on from his prison sentence for possession, his appetite for pot was as strong as ever. He sat quietly in the corner of the room watching the monitor on which the show was being screened and grew progressively more stoned. By the time the floor manager came in to prepare him for the big surprise climax to the show he was in a world of his own.

Nevertheless, he was taken into the wings and told that his cue to walk on was when the show's host, Bruce Forsyth, said: 'And here, flown in especially from the United States, Hollywood legend Robert Mitchum.'

He was still smoking his pipe until a health-and-safety official insisted that he put it out. Mitchum tucked it into his top pocket, and dreamily watched Bruce going through some banter with the audience. He listened hard for his name. Incredibly, though, Bruce had one of his rare lapses and started to wind up the show without announcing that Mitchum was there. 'Thanks for watching, and it was nice to see you, to see you nice,' he declared in his traditional sign-off.

The purple-faced floor manager was waving his arms like a demented tic-tac man to tell Bruce that the final award had to be made to Mitchum, who was still looking on blankly, perhaps wondering if he had already been on and come off.

Bruce quickly started doing what he does best, ad-libbing his way out of trouble. 'But before we go, one last great surprise,' he said to the confused audience. 'Flown in especially from the United States, Hollywood legend Robert Mitchum.'

A quick shove in the back from the floor manager sent an almost comatose Mitchum on to the stage. He was given his award and barely mumbled a thank-you before the closing titles were up and running.

Just as the commercials were about to start, Mitchum could be heard saying: 'Is that it?'

I know I've shared that story before, but I reckon it's always worth repeating. For all his drinking, hell-raising and womanising, Mitchum somehow remained married to the same woman, Dorothy, for fifty-seven years, until his death in 1997 at the age of seventy-nine.

'No matter what he got up to,' said Dorothy Mitchum, 'Bob always came back to me and the kids. He knew his place.'

8 Clark Gable Always a heavy drinker from his days as an oilrig worker, the 'King of Hollywood' became awash with whiskey following the death in a 1942 air crash of the third of his five wives, Carole Lombard. For a long time afterwards he rarely knew a sober day as he looked for a way through his grief at the bottom of a glass. It was strongly rumoured that his studio had hushed up the fact that he had killed a woman pedestrian while drunk at the wheel of his car in 1945, at the peak of his popularity.

Things were never quite what they seemed with Gable. Even those gleaming teeth of his were false. He had all his original gnashers removed in 1933 after suffering from gum disease.

Writer Anita Loos (who penned *Gentlemen Prefer Blondes*) revealed how she had once seen Gable without his teeth. 'I most admired Clark for his lack of vanity,' she said. 'One day I happened on him as he stood washing his dentures. Clark grinned, pointed to his caved-in mouth and said with an exaggerated lisp, "Look, America'th Thweetheart."'

It is hard for younger generations to realise just how massive a star Gable was, but he was certainly far bigger than any of today's screen idols. During his Oscar-winning performance in the 1934 film *It Happened One Night*, in one scene he took off his shirt to reveal he was not wearing a vest. The American underwear industry went into free-fall because suddenly nobody was buying vests!

His drinking sprees in the company of the likes of Bogart, David Niven and actor/director John Huston are the stuff of Hollywood legend. It was nothing for them to sit right through the night playing poker and getting pie-eyed.

When he made *Gone with the Wind* in 1939 the six-foot-one Gable was a muscular fourteen stone; but years of hard drinking saw him tip the scales at a flabby seventeen stone in the fifties. For his final film, *The Misfits*, he went on a severe, pill-popping diet to get back into his pre-war shape. This, rather than his drinking, is believed to have contributed to his death before the film was released in 1960.

His co-star in *The Misfits* was Marilyn Monroe. It would be her last completed film, too. The screenplay was by her husband Arthur Miller, and the film was shot while their marriage was falling apart. She threw tantrums throughout the filming, often failed to show up for scenes, and struggled to remember her lines. Eventually, Gable grew so frustrated that he dismissed his double and began doing his own stunts, including a scene in which he was dragged across the desert behind a truck.

He said he did it himself because he wanted to blow off steam after being kept hanging around waiting for Marilyn to show up. 'I'm glad this picture's finished,' a bruised and bloody Gable told a friend after the wrap. 'Marilyn damn near gave me a heart attack.'

Two days later, while changing a tyre on his station wagon, the King of Hollywood keeled over with a massive coronary. He died the following week at the age of just fifty-nine.

His old drinking partner John Huston had been the director of *The Misfits*. On hearing the news of Gable's death, he said: 'If Clark and I had our lives to live over again, I think we would learn the joys of wine instead of hard liquor.'

Frankly, I don't think Clark Gable could have given a damn.

7 William Holden Clark Gable's death may not have been directly related to alcohol, but that of another fine actor, William Holden, certainly was. He fell over during a solo binge at his home in 1981, struck his head on a coffee table and was so intoxicated that he did not realise he was badly injured. Forensic evidence at his inquest proved that he lived for thirty minutes after his fall, and if he had called for help during that time he could well have been saved. It seems he was simply too drunk to bother.

Loretta Young warned a young Holden that he should keep his drinking under control after starring with him and Robert Mitchum in the 1948 film *Rachel and the Stranger*. She left the two actors sitting downstairs in her rented house and went to bed because of an early morning shoot. When she got up the next day they were sitting in the same seats absolutely plastered, with two empty bottles of whiskey on the table between them. Young later revealed: 'I told them they were going to become big stars for years to come, but that they would not enjoy it if they turned into drunks.'

Holden made many excellent films after this episode, winning an Oscar for his role in *Stalag 17* and gaining acclaim for his performances in *Picnic, Born Yesterday, Sunset Boulevard, The Wild Bunch, Bridge over the River Kwai* and *Network*. But all the time he was getting deeper into the vodka bottle, as an extraordinary incident in Hong Kong the year before his death reveals. He remembered drinking a glass of wine at the start of a meal and coming round in his hotel bed several days later. But he didn't have a clue what he had been up to in between. He had managed to drink away a whole week. A month later he was at home in California when several hugely expensive Buddha statues were delivered to his door. He had apparently ordered them during his drunken adventure in Hong Kong.

Holden said that he lost much of his motivation for acting after winning his Oscar in 1953 ('How do I follow that?'), so he decided to take on roles purely for the money, often demanding ridiculously inflated fees, which were frequently paid by studios eager to have such an acclaimed actor on board. For *Bridge over the River Kwai* he asked for what was then a colossal one million dollars *plus* a percentage of profits. As usual, the film company coughed up.

He was basically a shy man who especially hated dancing, so he plotted to get a dance scene with Kim Novak written out of the film *Picnic*. He demanded eight thousand dollars' 'stunt man' money in the belief that the producers would be so outraged that they would cut the scene. But they paid up, and Bill and Kim produced one of the sexiest dance scenes ever screened. (Blimey, I would have volunteered to be his stunt double for it!)

His last great performance was in *Network* in 1976, for which he received an Oscar nomination while co-stars Peter Finch and Faye Dunaway both won Academy Awards. Finch, one of the few actors who could match Holden in the drinking stakes, died before the ceremony.

After *Network*, though, Holden got lost in a boozing maze and did much of his drinking alone. Few people realised how serious his problem had become until it was too late. He died aged just sixty-three, proving once again that while booze can be fun, it can also kill.

6 Judy Garland Exceptional talent and extreme vulnerability combined to make Judy Garland one of the most enduringly popular Hollywood icons of the twentieth century. But she was also one of the saddest. Judy was found dead in the bathroom of her rented Chelsea home by her fifth and last husband, Mickey Deans, in the summer of 1969, just a week after her forty-seventh birthday. The coroner ruled that she had died from an accidental overdose of sleeping pills.

Several times in her life she had attempted to commit suicide as she tried to cope with weight problems, lack of sleep, loss of confidence, marriage break-ups, black depressions and a growing dependence on drugs and alcohol. She seemed to lose everything but her talent.

Forever remembered as Dorothy in *The Wizard of Oz*, she had a dual career as an actress and singer who could hold an audience in the palm of her hand. But she could not hold her drink.

As she approached middle age and after four failed marriages, she became compelling viewing in the United States as she turned up for a succession of TV chat and variety shows obviously under the influence of booze and pills.

Entertainer Mel Tormé, who had been a child star in the same stable as Garland and Mickey Rooney, gave a glimpse into Judy's crazy grown-up world after he had performed on her *Christmas Special* television show in 1964. According to Tormé's memoirs, Judy had been on a drinking binge the night before and nobody could find her. The producers were just about to pull the plug with a few hours to go to airtime when she was found in a heavily intoxicated state. Lashings of hot coffee and medication were poured down her throat to get her ready for a hasty rehearsal and then the recording of the show.

'As Judy went through her paces in the studio, I could only look at her and marvel,' Tormé said on a 1970 chat show. 'How she had managed to return home, change clothes, do whatever she had to do to drag herself out of the sleepless abyss she must have been in and show up all within the course of an hour and a half was completely beyond me. Yet here she was, alert, alive, energetic, looking frighteningly normal. I thought of a description I had once heard of her, "The Concrete Canary", and once again I realised how it fitted her.'

The girl who had started out in life as Frances Ethel Gumm had been a victim of the Hollywood studio system. In the 1930s, hoping to keep her weight down, MGM chief Louis B. Mayer ordered the studio canteen to serve her nothing but chicken soup. When the naturally chubby teenager continued to balloon, MGM persuaded doctors to prescribe a cocktail of amphetamines and sleep-inducing sedatives. Unsurprisingly, she was addicted to the tablets before she was out of her teens, and found the only escape from her rollercoaster moods in the bottom of a glass.

But it wasn't until 1950 that it became public knowledge that twenty-nine-year-old Judy's drinking and pill-popping were out of control. Well-founded gossip got into the newspapers that she was staggering and falling down on the set of *Annie Get Your Gun*. The studio showed her no mercy and she was replaced in the title role by Betty Hutton, even though Judy had already recorded the entire soundtrack.

Soon afterwards she locked herself in a bathroom, broke a mirror and tried to kill herself, but she was saved before she could do serious damage.

Some time later, she received a get-well message from fellow-MGM star Katharine Hepburn: 'I can think of many singers who should cut their throat, but so glad that you failed.'

A little film trivia for you . . . Judy was not the original choice for her most famous role, Dorothy in *The Wizard of Oz*. She got the part only because Fox Studios refused to release Shirley Temple, who at the time was nine years old, the age of Dorothy in the original script. So the seventeen-year-old Judy was shoe-horned into the role, but she never did see the other side of that rainbow.

5 Richard Harris This affable Irishman went through life like a two-fisted hurricane, acting and singing his way to fame and fortune, but collecting lots of headlines and hangovers along the way. He was proud to carry on the tradition of Hollywood hellraisers, and officially passed the baton on to Russell Crowe after they had worked together on *Gladiator*.

Not long before his death in 2002, Harris said: 'Russell is a top bloke, loves his rugby, doesn't give a stuff, is a brilliant actor and

Richard Harris
collected headlines
and hangovers with
his hellraising.

a much-loved new friend. He irritates the hell out of the Hollywood bigwigs, but he's much too good for them to ignore.'

He could have been talking about himself. He certainly had much too much talent for Hollywood to ignore, and he was always in demand as a box-office magnet, despite his reputation for being exceptionally hot to handle.

Just to give you an idea of his drinking capacity, whenever he visited New York, he would go straight to P.J. Clarke's bar and demand 'my usual' from the regular barman, Vinnie, who would place six double vodkas on the bar.

Harris became such a close pal of Vinnie that he was put in charge one night while the bartender went to a ball game. It was like putting a drunken clown in charge of a circus. 'I almost ruined the business in one mad night,' Harris recalled some years later. 'I was giving drinks away to customers because I could not bring myself to ask for their money. When I started getting the big film parts I sent the owner a cheque to make up for the night I gave all his booze away. I'm told it was one helluva night.'

Starring in Brendan Behan's *The Quare Fellow* at the Stratford East Theatre in London, the young Richard Harris met up with his best friend – another rising actor called Peter O'Toole – for an after-show drink. Eight hours later they arrived back at their digs aboard a milk float. 'I've no idea where we've been but I think we've had a great time,' Harris told legendary Stratford East producer Joan Littlewood. 'I think you could say we were *two* quare fellows.'

Joan said, very prophetically: 'Richard will develop into a great actor, and he is going to make friends with a lot of barmen along the way.'

He made no secret of the fact that he was happy to be pigeon-holed as a hellraiser. 'There are too many prima donnas in this business and not enough action,' he once remarked. 'Life is there to be lived to the full.'

Late in his career he found a whole new generation of fans with his portrayal of Professor Albus Dumbledore, headmaster of

Hogwarts School. 'My granddaughter said she'd never talk to me again unless I took the part,' he admitted.

He had no time for the modern star system. 'What I hate about our business today is the elitism,' he once said. 'So-called stars ride in private jets and have bodyguards and dieticians and beauticians. Tom Cruise is a midget and he has eight bodyguards all six feet ten, which makes him look even more diminutive. It's an absolute joke.'

That was Richard Harris, who pulled no punches but had plenty of pints pulled for him during his rumbustious life.

4 W.C. Fields When I used to get prepared for my portrayal of Jim Royle, I used to tell the make-up girl to give me 'a W.C. Fields' nose. He had a real boozer's conk, and as he got deeper into the gin bottle his nose became more and more of a beacon signalling the sort of life he was leading.

He eventually had a medical condition named after him – 'W.C. Fields syndrome' – characterised by rhinophyma (a skin infection on the nose and abnormal growth) and often associated with alcoholism.

Fields was a comedy genius, coming from the world of silent movies and – before that – vaudeville, where he was a master juggler making deliberate mistakes. He would reprimand a particular ball which had not come to his hand accurately, slap his battered silk hat for not staying on his head, and mutter weird and unintelligible expletives to his cigar when it missed his mouth.

Born William Claude Dukenfield in 1880 in Pennsylvania, he made the transition from the silent screen to talkies, and became a huge star with films like *My Little Chickadee*, *Never Give a Sucker an Even Break* and *The Bank Dick*. He stole the film with an unforgettable performance as Mr Micawber in *David Copperfield*. Amazingly, he was fifty before he made his first talkie, yet he achieved enough over the following fifteen years to become a Hollywood legend.

Away from the stage and screen Fields had a reputation for heavy boozing ('I never drink water because of the disgusting things that fish do in it'). His publicists insisted that a lot of his drinking was all part of the act, but it was reported that in the last week of his life he had a crate of gin secretly smuggled to his bedside.

As my little tribute to this master of comedy, here are my favourite W.C. Fields drink-related quotes:

'How well I remember my first encounter with the Devil's Brew. I happened to stumble across a case of bourbon – and went right on stumbling for several days thereafter.'

'Now don't say you can't swear off drinking. It's easy. I did it last night, and I'll do it again tomorrow night.'

'Thou shalt not covet thy neighbour's house unless they have a well-stocked bar.'

'Somebody's spiked my drink with pineapple juice!'

'What would my father think of me consuming two quarts of liquor a day? He'd think I was a sissy.'

'I exercise extreme self-control. I never drink anything stronger than gin before breakfast.'

'I don't believe in dining on an empty stomach.'

'Some weasel took the cork out of my lunch.'

'I never drank anything stronger than beer before I was twelve.'

'I seldom took a drink on the set before nine a.m.'

'I certainly do not drink all the time. I have to sleep, you know.'

'A woman drove me to drink, and I'm ashamed to say that I never even had the courtesy to thank her.'

'It's been suggested that one day I will drown in a vat of whiskey. Oh death, where is thy sting?'

'During one of my treks through Afghanistan, we lost our corkscrew. We were compelled to live on food and water for several days.'

'Christmas at my house is always at least six or seven times more pleasant than anywhere else. We start drinking early. And while everyone else is seeing only one Santa Claus, we'll be seeing six or seven.'

W.C. Fields. There will never be another like him.

3 Robert Newton 'Pissed as a Newton' became a phrase among actors when the one and only Robert Newton was at his paralytic peak. His drinking damaged him hugely, and a highly erratic stage and film career was the result. He often found himself unemployable due to his unreliability.

Yet more than sixty years on we still mimic his unforgettable 'Aggh, Jim lad' line from his towering performance as Long John Silver in *Treasure Island*.

The West Country accent came easily to him. He was born in delightful Dorset in 1905 and died just fifty years later in Beverly Hills of a heart attack, almost certainly brought on by excessive drinking.

There are dozens of Newton anecdotes that live on in the acting profession, many of them apocryphal, but I like to think there's some basis of truth to them. My favourite features another famous drunk, Wilfrid Lawson, when both actors appeared in *Richard III*. They shared a heavy liquid lunch before a matinée performance and arrived at the theatre in a legless condition.

Lawson stumbled on in the title role and was slurring his way through the opening soliloquy when a member of the audience shouted, 'You're drunk, sir!' Summoning all the dignity he could muster, Lawson stared in the direction of his heckler and said, 'You think *I'm* drunk? Wait till you see Buckingham!' Played, of course, by Newton.

For all his boozing, Newton never lost the charm that could win friends and influence people in the film industry. The great director David Lean, who was known for his puritanical attitude towards drinking and dislike of actors in general, worked with Newton on *Oliver Twist*, *This Happy Breed* and *Major Barbara* and was very fond of him. He once said:

> *I had a great weakness for Bobby Newton. He used to drink far too much. And when he had a couple of drinks he would speak the absolute truth, which could be horrifying. I remember him talking to a friend of mine after lunch, when he'd had a couple of drinks, and he leaned across the table and said, 'Now I'm going to tell you about you.' And he did, bang, on the nose, you know. Withering. He could be cruel, but what he said was undeniably true. I loved him.*

His long-time drinking partner and close pal David Niven (who just failed to make this list!) said of Newton's capacity for alcohol:

> *With just the right amount on board he could be fascinating but once he had taken the extra one he changed gear and would become anything from unpredictable to a downright menace. Along with his wife, we all tried loyally and desperately to help him, but his charm was so great and, when he took only a couple of drinks, his entertainment value was so spectacular that there was always some idiot who would press him to take the fatal third and fourth glass.*

In 1955, Newton landed what proved to be his final role, as the Scotland Yard detective Inspector Fix in the Academy Award-winning *Around the World in Eighty Days*. Niven, who starred as Phileas Fogg, got his friend the job, as he recalled years later on a TV chat show:

It was all arranged for the Mexican bullfighter–comedian Cantinflas to play my valet, Passepartout, and Shirley MacLaine was signed for the part of Princess Aouda. The cast was heaving with stars of the calibre of Noël Coward, Charles Boyer, Red Skelton, Ronald Colman, Frank Sinatra and John Gielgud.

Our larger-than-life producer Mike Todd for some reason had a complete blank as to who could play the important part of Inspector Fix. As Mike sat chomping on his cigar, I suddenly had the brainwave that it was ideal for my dear friend Bob Newton. He had been having a bit of a rough time of it because of his well-known problem with the old hooch, but I was convinced he could do the job.

'How about Robert Newton?' I suggested. Todd was immediately enchanted with the idea and put in a call.

As he was dialling the number I suddenly realised the dangers, and felt a bit of a heel as I warned Mike: 'Bob's a great friend of mine, but he does drink a lot these days and you must protect yourself. Lots of people are scared to employ him. He, uh, sort of disappears.'

'I am going to arrange to see Newton,' Mike said firmly, 'and when he comes in, I want you here in the office with us.'

I nearly had kittens. 'Please, Mike, don't tell him I said anything,' I begged. 'Bobby will never forgive me.'

The next day I was summoned into Mike's office and Bobby came shuffling in after me. I hadn't seen him for a couple of months and it was obvious he'd been on an almighty binge. Glowing nose, inane grin, crumpled clothes.

Todd ignored his dishevelled state. 'Ever heard of Jules Verne?' he asked.

'Ah, dear fellow,' said Newton. 'What a wordsmith!'

'Eighty Days around the World?'

'A glorious piece, old cock.'

'How'd you like to play Inspector Fix?'

'A splendid role,' said Robert, rolling those expressive eyes of his. 'Do I understand you are offering it to me, dear boy?'

'I might,' said Todd, then pointing at me and making me feel like something that had just crawled in under the door. 'But your pal Niven, here, says you're a lush.'

'Aah!' said Bobby. 'My pal Niven has always been a master of the understatement.'

Todd roared with laughter, taken in by Bobby's natural charm and wit. He was immediately hired and gave his word of honour to Todd that he would go on the wagon for the duration of the picture. He stuck to his promise, and gave a wonderful performance.

There is a punchline. While working on location, Bobby and I used to go fishing by moonlight in the mountain lakes. As we sat side-by-side on the boat, Bobby confessed to me that his promise to Todd had not really been all that difficult to give. The very morning of that meeting in Mike's office his doctor had warned him that one more alcoholic session would almost certainly be fatal. I was so pleased that my friend had heeded the warning and had sworn off drinking for life.

Two weeks after we finished the picture, Todd called a few of us back for an added scene on a ship. Bobby was required for only one day, but when he arrived on the set, a roaring delivery of 'Once more unto the breach . . .' announced alarming news: our hero was spectacularly off the wagon. 'Oh, Bobby,' I said, 'what have you done to yourself?'

He put his arm around my neck and, with tears rolling down his swollen cheeks, said: 'Don't chide me, dear fellow, please don't chide me.'

It was the last time I saw him. Within a few days, the doctor's warning proved tragically correct.

On 25 March 1956, Robert Newton died in the arms of his wife Vera. What could have been one of the greatest of all acting careers had been drowned in a sea of alcohol. Agggh, Robert Lad, how different it all might have been if you had learned to refuse the next drink.

2 Richard Burton The son of a Welsh coalminer, Richard Burton escaped the pits to become one of the world's great actors. Sadly, he also became one of the world's great piss artists.

He had the talent to become as respected as Olivier, Gielgud or Richardson – his heroes – but somewhere along the way he got lost in the bottle, and he is now more likely to be remembered for his turbulent personal life and multiple marriages than as 'The Voice' of stage and screen.

He was born Richard Jenkins in the village of Pontrhydyfen, South Wales, in 1925, the twelfth of thirteen children. His mother died when he was just two years old, and the family had to borrow the ten pounds needed to pay for the funeral.

He spoke no English up to the age of ten, when he started to be tutored by a schoolmaster named Philip Burton, who subsequently became his guardian. As well as teaching him English, Philip Burton showed young Richard how to hold a knife and fork correctly and educated him in the classics. He also gave him an all-consuming desire for knowledge, so throughout his life Richard remained an avid reader. ('Home', he used to say, 'is where the books are.')

He won a scholarship to Oxford University, where he studied literature . . . and learned how to sink a pint of beer in seven seconds.

After Second World War service in the Royal Air Force as a navigator he resumed a fledgling acting career, and by the time he was into his late twenties he had won acclaim as one of Britain's greatest Shakespearean stage actors.

He had rugged good looks to go with a magnetic stage presence and an incomparable voice. Just ordering from the menu, he could sound like a Welsh rhapsody. Even Richard himself would talk about 'the Burton voice' in the third person as if it were a gift from the theatrical gods.

But even in those early days of fame he was looked on as a 'troubled spirit' who was such a perfectionist that if the slightest thing went wrong he would reach for the bottle for consolation. Sir John Gielgud was moved to say that Richard should have been in the same rank as Laurence Olivier, 'but he was very wild and had a scandal around him all the time and I think in theatre circles that would not be approved of'.

His career was crazily erratic. He was the most nominated actor never to win an Oscar (seven nominations) and the most famous British actor who was never knighted. He made more than forty movies, ranging from such classics as *My Cousin Rachel*, *Who's Afraid of Virginia Woolf?*, *The Spy Who Came in from the Cold*, *Anne of the Thousand Days* and *Becket* to a string of forgotten failures to which he should never have lent his name or his talent.

His fame transcended the film world when he started a headline-hitting affair with Elizabeth Taylor during the making of the blockbuster *Cleopatra*. Suddenly the name Burton was internationally known, including by Taylor's then husband, the singer Eddie Fisher. He telephoned his wife to see what was going on and Burton answered the phone. 'What are you doing with my wife?' Fisher asked. 'I'm f****** her, what d'you think?' came the response.

As the story and the scandal grew, Laurence Olivier sent a cable to Burton that read: 'Make up your mind, dear heart, do you want to be a great actor or a household word?'

Burton sent back a one-word reply: 'Both.'

On Broadway, his performances in *Hamlet*, *Camelot* and *Equus* received rave reviews, but his double-hander with Elizabeth Taylor in *Private Lives* was, many critics felt, too close to their stormy romance for comfort.

As the pressures of fame intensified, Burton developed a self-destructive streak that manifested itself in bouts of prolonged drinking. He once drank a quart of brandy *during* a performance of *Hamlet* on

Broadway. 'The only visible effect', according to fellow-actor James Bacon, 'was that he played the last two acts as a homosexual.'

While playing King Arthur in *Camelot*, Burton regularly indulged in vodka. He once downed a bottle during a matinée and a second during the evening performance (and went on to win a Tony Award for the role).

'When I played drunks I had to remain sober,' he said, 'because I didn't know how to play them when I was drunk. But playing somebody sober while drunk has never been a problem for me.'

In a 1974 interview, he said: 'I was up to – I'm told, because, of course, you don't remember if you drink that much – about two and a half to three bottles of hard liquor a day. Fascinating idea, of course, drink on that scale. It's rather nice to have gone through it and to have survived.'

Many feel that it was the theatre's loss that Burton squandered his energy on second-rate films, five marriages – two of them to Elizabeth Taylor – and all of those legendary bouts with the bottle. He boasted, earlier in his career, about being able to drink half-gallons of cognac or 100-proof vodka during stage performances, and he was renowned as a womaniser.

'He has a terrific way with women,' Fredric March said after they had made *Alexander the Great* together. 'I don't think he has missed more than half a dozen.'

When he reached the age of fifty, after a five-year career slump, Burton called his own life the best role he had ever played. He said with heavy irony: 'I rather like my reputation, actually, that of a spoiled genius from the Welsh gutter, a drunk, a womaniser. It's rather an attractive image.'

In one of his last major interviews, he was still insisting, 'I can only say with Edith Piaf, "*Je ne regrette rien*."'

But the acting profession and his legions of fans certainly had deep regrets when he died of a cerebral haemorrhage in Switzerland in 1984. He was fifty-eight years old.

Errol Flynn, the most notorious of the legless legends of Hollywood, parties with Shelley Winters.

1 Errol Flynn Swashbuckling on screen and through life, Errol Flynn became a (legless) legend with adventures that made him *the* Don Juan of the twentieth century.

Born in Tasmania at the bottom of the world, he rose to the top. But when he reached the peak of his career he made headlines more for his behaviour off the screen than for his performances on it.

He was the son of Theodore Thomas Flynn (a noted biologist) and Marrelle Young Flynn, who was descended from Fletcher Christian of HMS *Bounty* fame. In his early years, the family relocated back to England, where Flynn, a hyperactive child, managed to get into trouble and thrown out of every school he attended.

When he finally completed his severely interrupted education, he worked in a series of odd jobs, never keeping one more than a few months. He tried the tobacco plantation business and failed, then went into copper mining but quickly decided it was not for him. Along the way he had a series of flings that made him the target for a queue of jealous husbands. To avoid their wrath he returned to Australia, where he stumbled into acting, playing the role of his ancestor Fletcher Christian in the 1933 film *In the Wake of the Bounty*.

His good looks and natural athletic ability brought him to the notice of Warner Brothers after he had returned to England to start a stage career, and he was offered a job in Hollywood. After several bit parts, he landed the title role in 1935's *Captain Blood*, and his screen chemistry with Olivia de Havilland (in the first of eight films with her) had the critics hailing him as the 'new Rudolph Valentino'.

But he became typecast in sword-play films, and grew frustrated that his acting talents were being buried inside scripts that called for him to do little more than swing from ships' masts or between trees in Sherwood Forest.

By now his off-screen exploits were getting him more attention as he attempted to drink California dry and consistently proved himself a skilled swordsman of a different kind. 'I like my whisky old and my women young,' he said.

But then it sensationally emerged that perhaps he liked his women too young. In November 1942, he was arrested and tried for statutory rape after two teenage girls claimed that he had seduced them when they were under the age of consent. The trial was so big that it even pushed news of the Second World War off the front pages. Obviously this was an immensely serious episode for all involved, but the proceedings were not without their humorous moments. Courtroom observers chortled, for example, when one of the girls recalled Flynn's 'come-on-below' line during their tryst aboard his yacht: 'Darling,' she quoted him as saying, 'that moon would look even more beautiful through a porthole.'

Flynn famously downed five shots of vodka before taking the

stand, denied everything, and was promptly acquitted. He was also immortalised, because of the speed with which he bedded women, in a new phrase that made worldwide headlines: 'In like Flynn.'

Rather than destroy his career, the scandal strengthened his image with the public. In later years, his drinking, wenching and love of the wild life began to catch up with him, but he was finally allowed to prove he could really act, playing an alcoholic in *The Sun Also Rises* (1957) and the alcoholic actor John Barrymore in *Too Much, Too Soon* (1958).

His final years were spent on his yacht, *Zaca*, in Port Antonio, Jamaica, where he worked on his posthumously published auto-biography, the appropriately titled *My Wicked Wicked Ways*.

He was controversial to the end, getting emotionally involved with a fifteen-year-old student and grooming her for a planned marriage. He died in her arms following a heart attack during an impromptu party in 1959. He was sixty years old.

To keep him company on his final journey, six bottles of whisky were placed in his coffin. His last words were reported to have been: 'I've had a hell of a lot of fun and I've enjoyed every minute of it.'

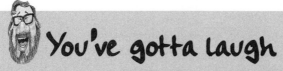# You've gotta laugh

A former heavyweight wrestler opened a pub, and to attract custom he offered a thousand pounds to anybody who could beat him in 'a squeezing contest'.

He would hold a lemon in his right hand and squeeze and squeeze until there did not seem to be any juice left. Any customer who could squeeze one more drop out of the lemon would collect the money.

Challengers came from far and wide to try to win the thousand pounds. They included weightlifters, burly lorry drivers, shotputters, bodybuilders, navvies, coalmen, meat porters and rugby forwards. All of them failed to get any more out of the lemon.

Then, one evening, a skinny little man in a raincoat and wearing thick-rimmed glasses came in and asked if he could take the challenge.

The publican waited for the laughter of the other customers to die down before agreeing to let the bloke take him on in the squeezing contest.

He did his usual thorough squeezing job on a lemon and squirted the contents into a glass. He then handed what was left of the lemon to the little man.

Without even taking off his raincoat, the scrawny man promptly squeezed six more drops of lemon juice on to the bar.

Everyone looked on in amazement as the landlord handed over the prize money.

'What do you do for a living that has given you such strength?' the publican asked as he counted out the cash. 'Are you on steroids or something?'

'No,' the little man replied, 'I work for the Inland Revenue.'

Hark Who's Talking About Drink

'A hangover is the wrath of grapes.'
- **Denis Goodwin**

'I tried hard to drown my sorrows but they are strong swimmers.'
- **Spike Milligan**

'One reason I don't drink is that I want to know when I am having a good time.'
- **Lady Astor**

'My body is a temple, and it feels good to have spirits inside it.'
- **Dave Allen**

'I like liquor – its taste and its effects. And that is just the reason why I never drink it.'
- **Thomas Jackson**

'I complained to the publican when he doubled the prices during what should have been the happy hour. "How can you call this a happy hour?" I asked. He replied: "Well, it makes me happy."'
- **John Edwards**

'My grandmother is over eighty and still doesn't need glasses. Drinks right out of the bottle.'
- **Henny Youngman**

'My mother-in-law drinks like a fish. She doesn't order by pints but by gills.'
- **Les Dawson**

'The worst three words in the English language when strung together – "Last orders please."'
- **Johnny Speight**

'I amazed everybody by ordering our drinks in fluent French. We were in a Chinese restaurant at the time.'
- **Tommy Cooper**

The Sporting Best of Times

8

When I was a youngster just falling in love with everything sporting (with football and boxing at the top of my list), it was an unwritten law that professional sportsmen should be sober, early-to-bed individuals who would faint at the sniff of a barmaid's apron.

Our heroes, giants of sport like Stanley Matthews, Tom Finney, Billy Wright, Billy Liddell, Len Hutton, Don Bradman, Bruce Woodcock and Rocky Marciano, were all virtually teetotal and you never saw their names in the headlines for boozing misdemeanours.

What a change I've witnessed over the years! You can hardly open a newspaper these days without finding a sports star up to his neck in scandal, which usually involves the demon drink. But as hard as a lot of them seem to be trying, I don't think any of them will be able to match the Irish imp George Best for roller-coaster adventures off the pitch.

'If I'd been born ugly,' George once said, 'you would never have heard of Pelé.'

It's true that his babe-magnet good looks led him into more bedroom romps than most of us have had hot toast (George preferred crumpet). But it was his insatiable thirst that really proved his Achilles heel and put lead into his flying boots. If George had been able to pass a pub like he passed a ball then he would have been right up there with Pelé and Maradona instead of just a short head behind. (Although the little Argentinian has hardly been a model of sobriety himself!)

Best's style of play was breathtaking and unique, featuring a repertoire of feints and swerves, unexpected stops and sudden spurts, which left opponents bemused and bewildered. Despite his slight build, he had tremendous physical strength and resilience, and he could ghost past tight-marking defenders as if they were not there. Paddy Crerand, Best's Manchester United team-mate, summed it up beautifully when he said that he gave opponents 'twisted blood'.

But George was drawn to the high life like a wasp to a jam pot. And hell's bells, he really got stuck in. With all that natural physical grace and his stunning looks, he became the first British sportsman to be accorded pop-star status. Blimey, even I fancied him!

Throughout the mid-to-late sixties his photograph was as likely to be seen in the music press as on the sports pages. He was an icon – the 'Fifth Beatle'. There was always a blonde (or two) by his side, but out of sight were the drinks that he would consume with an ever-increasing desire. Eventually, they would consume him.

It hurts me as a red-blooded Scouser to have to admit that in the sixties, when George, Bobby Charlton and Denis Law were at their peak, Manchester United were far and away the finest team in England; and possibly in the world. They won the League Championship twice and in 1968 became the first English club to capture the European Cup.

And Bestie, European Footballer of the Year that season, was at the heart of it all.

They were the good times for George. But the bad times were waiting just around the corner. As the seventies dawned, he became disillusioned and depressed, a dangerous combination for a potential alcoholic. His Manchester United career ended prematurely and controversially in his mid-twenties, and his drink-fuelled behaviour became increasingly erratic.

George Best: 'I spent all my money on wine and women, and the rest I squandered.'

We looked on helplessly, as if seeing our best friend driving the wrong way down a motorway. A lot of people tried to point him in the right direction, but he would not listen or learn. A crash was inevitable. Bored and despondent, he wasted his time and talent in a mindless round of womanising and drinking. 'I spent most of my money on wine and women,' he joked on the chat-show circuit. 'The rest I squandered.'

But he also lost his self-respect, many of the friends who cared about him, and that yard of pace that had set him aside from mere mortals on the football pitch.

In 1976 he joined other ageing icons, such as Pelé, Franz Beckenbauer and Bobby Moore, in the circus of the North American League, first for the Los Angeles Aztecs and later for San Jose. He enjoyed the anonymity of life in California, but it became more a theatre of nightmares than of dreams.

He married Angie MacDonald James, a former Bunnygirl, but the relationship folded under the weight of his alcoholism and serial unfaithfulness. They separated soon after George was hospitalised as a result of his addiction.

After returning to Britain, he had brief spells playing for Fulham and for Hibernian in Scotland. But he was a shadow (albeit an increasingly chubby one) of the player who had thrilled millions at the peak of his powers. After his final retirement, he spent long periods lost in an alcoholic haze.

The sad headlines, whether for bankruptcy or imprisonment on a drink-driving and assault charge, continued, but in spite of his alcoholism George occasionally appeared to be at peace with himself. And he seemed genuinely happy in his second marriage to Alex Pursey, a former air hostess (although they divorced in 2004).

In 2002 he had the good fortune to be given a liver transplant. Those of us who loved him looked forward to a happy ending to the astonishing George Best Story. But, ignoring a crescendo of public criticism, he went back on the bottle after being given a golden second chance of life, and paid the ultimate penalty when he died in Cromwell Hospital in November 2005, aged fifty-nine.

It was a tragedy in so many ways, but nobody will ever be able to erase the memories of George purring through defences like a Rolls-Royce going past dustcarts. He was the greatest of sights when in full flow on the football pitch, the only place where he was ever truly in control of himself.

Out of respect to the memory of the greatest of all British footballers, here's my favourite story about him. I heard George himself tell it many times, but it never ceases to amuse.

In typical George fashion, he was dating Miss World. One night he took her to a casino and won twenty grand with a single spin of the roulette wheel. With the winnings stashed into his pockets and with officially the world's most beautiful woman on his arm, he took a chauffeured limousine back to the Manchester hotel where they were staying.

As the wizened little Irish night porter let them in, George tipped him twenty quid to bring a bottle of chilled Dom Perignon up to their room.

Miss World, in a see-through negligée, was just coming out of the bathroom and the twenty grand was spread over the bed when the porter arrived with the champagne.

As he put the tray on the bedside table, the porter asked a little nervously, 'I wonder, George, if you mind a fellow-Ulsterman putting a personal question to you?'

'Fire away,' said George, peeling off another tenner from the stack of money and handing it to his countryman.

'I was just wondering,' said the porter, 'where did it all go wrong?'

Simply the Best.

Andrew 'Freddie' Flintoff, the greatest all-round English cricketer of his generation, has shown signs of having a George Best-style self-destruct button in his personality. And it's the old curse of alcohol that's at the heart of it.

He got into hot water (well, lukewarm at least) during the Cricket World Cup in the Caribbean in March 2007. There were reports of high jinks in a nightclub in St Lucia in the early hours of the morning after a six-wicket defeat by New Zealand and with another crucial match against Canada just around the corner. Several of the England players were so pissed that witnesses talked of them kissing each other and dancing on tables. Then Freddie took centre stage by nearly getting himself drowned. In his drunken stupor, he decided to take a pedalo out to sea. The little boat capsized, and he had to be hauled from the water.

To outsiders, the incident was hugely comical. But it was no laughing matter for Flintoff when he was stripped of the England vice-captaincy.

Of course, this was not the first time that Flintoff hogged the headlines with his boozing. The day after England's amazing Ashes victory against Australia in 2005 the undoubted hero of the hour came staggering out of the team hotel obviously well gone, and he was pictured wearing heavy-duty sunglasses on the bus during the victory parade through London. He said live on television: 'To be honest with you, I'm struggling. I've not been to bed yet and the eyes behind these glasses tell a thousand stories.'

As he walked unsteadily off the bus with an arm around team-mate Kevin Pietersen and went into No. 10, the word 'twat' was clearly emblazoned in felt-tip pen on his head. He later denied that it was he who had urinated in a flower bed in the Prime Minister's garden, although plenty of people still saw him as the chief suspect.

However, he did admit: 'I'd warned my wife Rachael what was likely to happen if we won, and she wisely went to bed and left me in the hotel bar. I had most of my closest mates there and I didn't want the night to end. I was drinking pints of Lancaster Bomber [a Blackburn-brewed beer]. I drank and drank and drank, before finally going up to my room around breakfast time to get ready for the reception we were due to have before we got into the open-top bus. I had a bath, put my blazer on and had another bottle of lager before we set off.'

We all felt it was a great laugh when he appeared legless on that occasion, so I suppose some double standards were applied when he was crucified eighteen months later for the pedalo incident. Are you supposed to drink only when you're winning? He was also vilified for allegedly getting hammered with the Barmy Army during the disastrous Ashes series in Oz just before the World Cup.

I sincerely hope Freddie follows the LBW rule with much of his future drinking – lots of bottled water. He is coming up to thirty, and is old and wise enough to know that he should be setting an example to the army of youngsters who look up to him as a role model. He is a magnificent cricketer, but booze does not distinguish between the good, the bad and the ugly. It can bowl them all over.

There was another cricketing Freddie making headlines for the wrong reasons long before Flintoff was even born. Fred Trueman was a legend in his own lifetime, the first bowler in the world to take three hundred Test wickets and a bloody-minded Yorkshireman who was continually at odds with the Establishment.

He was at his peak in a 'gentlemen and players' era when he was expected to be seen out on the pitch 'bowling his bollocks off' (Freddie's phrase, not mine) but not heard. However, Freddie had a mouth on him the size of Mars and was never frightened to offer an opinion or three.

It was unheard of to have an England cricketer with attitude, and the blazered MCC types punished him by repeatedly leaving him out of tour teams when it was obvious he was by far the finest of our quick bowlers. 'I'd have been the first bowler to take *six hundred* wickets, let alone three hundred, if they'd played me when they should have done,' Trueman was fond of reminding anybody who would listen.

Once, when sitting next to the Indian High Commissioner at an after-match banquet, Freddie was supposed to have said: 'Pass the salt, Gunga Din.' He always insisted that he said no such thing, but the selectors believed the story and used it against him, deciding he was too much of a loose cannon to allow on tour.

I loved the story Freddie told of a Yorkshire game against Northants in 1954 when Frank Tyson – one of the few to rival him as England's finest fast bowler – was ripping through the batting. 'Johnny Wardle were bowled all ends up by Tyson for nought,' Freddie recalled in after-dinner speeches that were the funniest on the circuit. '"A bloody fine shot that were," I told Johnny as we passed, him coming back to the pavilion and me on the way out to face Tyson. Well, it just so 'appened that I went first ball, too. "And a bloody fine shot that were, an' all," was Wardle's greeting to me as I got back to the hutch. But I were determined to have the last laugh. "Aye," I told him, "but I 'ad an excuse. I slipped on that pile o' sh*t you left in the crease."'

Trueman once bowled a Cambridge University batsman with a peach of a ball that ripped his middle stump out of the ground. 'Jolly fine ball,' said the Cambridge man in true Corinthian spirit as he walked past Freddie on his way back to the pavilion. 'Aye,' said our hero to his departing back, 'but it were wasted on you.'

It was rumoured that Freddie piled into the pints, but his partner Brian Statham was the real king in that department. He had hollow legs. Freddie often got sozzled, but gin and tonic eventually became his favourite tipple.

When he was knocking down wickets like ninepins on the county scene he thought nothing of going into the opposition dressing-room before play and saying, 'I need nine wickets from this match to improve my averages. You buggers had better start drawing straws to see who I don't get.'

Long before sledging became part and parcel of cricket, Freddie used to tell batsmen to f*** off when he thought he had them caught or leg before. And his stare after they had the temerity to score runs off him was cold enough to chill a hot curry.

During a tour Down Under, the England players were taken on a sightseeing trip through Sydney by an Australian cricket official. 'What do you think of our magnificent bridge?' the proud Aussie asked.

Ever the diplomat, Trueman responded: 'What do I think of your bridge? *Your* bridge? *Our* bloody bridge you should say. Bugger me, it were a Yorkshire firm – Dorman and Long – that built it. And you bastards still haven't paid for it.'

He was like a bull in a china shop in the *Test Match Special* commentary box, which had always previously been a genteel and gracious place. His favourite phrase, 'I don't know what's going off out there!' was directed disparagingly at a succession of modern England players he did not think were fit to lace his boots (or his drinks).

'Ian Botham couldn't bowl a hoop downhill,' he once said, ignoring the fact that Both was well on the way to taking seventy-six more Test wickets than Fred himself had.

Another classic: 'There's only one head bigger than Tony Greig's, and that's Birkenhead.'

A few years after he hung up his sweater he said: 'I've lost count of the number of times I was accused of drinking a couple of pints too many. I rarely drank beer but that didn't seem to stop the gossip. I've been seen dead drunk in places I've never visited, been seen escorting women I've never met and misbehaved in towns and on grounds I've never heard of.'

That's how legends become legends, I suppose.

To complete a hat-trick of Freds, we are joined by the spirit of the master tennis player Fred Perry, who remains the last British man to win a singles title at Wimbledon.

He was born in Stockport, the son of a Labour Member of Parliament. This was hardly the image for a player at Wimbledon, which in the 1930s was the snob capital of sport (with Henley, Lord's and Ascot all a short head behind).

'The members expected me to touch my forelock,' Perry recalled when attending the unveiling of a statue at Wimbledon to mark his feat of three successive titles on the Centre Court.

'They used to stand drinking their G and Ts and looking down their noses at me,' he said. 'I was a rebel from the wrong side of the tennis tramlines, and they just couldn't stomach the thought of this working-class boy walking off with their precious trophy.'

He looked at the statue showing him in majestic action and added: 'There will be a few former members of the All England Club and LTA revolving in their graves. They didn't even approve of me walking in through the front entrance. You ask Dan Maskell. He was official LTA coach here and had to use the tradesmen's entrance.'

No wonder Perry became a naturalised American. 'There's no class system over there,' he said. 'I was always made to feel like a second-class citizen in my playing days at Wimbledon.'

What a way to treat a hero. New balls, please.

Back to cricket and to one of the great characters who pioneered the sort of all-round game played by Freddie Flintoff. The one and only Ian Botham.

For those of you who were not around in the 1980s or were on another planet, I'd better remind you that 'Beefy' Botham was not merely the top English cricketer of the decade but the leading sports personality. He commanded endless newspaper headlines as his career touched improbable heights and bottomless depths. Within a year of first being picked for the England team in 1977 he was undisputed as the country's leading all-rounder. Within three years he was captain. Within four he had resigned (falling on his sword before being sacked), his form shot to pieces and having upset the pompous MCC members along the way to the point where there was a cold war between them and England's most talented player.

But then began the most famous comeback in English cricketing history, when Botham (now under Mike Brearley's captaincy) spurred England to an astonishing 1981 Ashes victory with three exhibitions – two with the bat, one with the ball – of out-of-this-world brilliance. Every one of his prodigious feats led to victory and he almost single-handedly inspired a boom in English cricket.

As he rattled off runs and skittled out batsmen Botham made no secret of his huge appetite for beer (although he is now a wine connoisseur), and that was acceptable while he did the business out

Man of many matches Ian Botham has walked the walk, talked the talk and has been rewarded with a well-deserved knighthood.

on the pitch. But when he drifted into the world of cannabis that was too much for his masters at Lord's and he was suspended.

Recalled against New Zealand for the 1986 Oval Test he took wickets with his first and twelfth balls to equal and then pass Dennis Lillee's old world record of 355 Test wickets. 'Who writes your scripts?' asked Graham Gooch. The big man just shrugged, grinned and then got on with the game.

Sledging (fielders trying to unsettle batsmen with insults) had now crept into the game, and boisterous Australian wicket-keeper Rodney Marsh tried to put Both off by asking: 'How's your wife and *my* kids?'

Completely unfazed, Botham replied: 'The wife's fine . . . the kids are retarded.'

Towards the end of his career, when he was combining cricket with pantomime appearances, Botham once rapped a batsman on the pads and shouted: ''Owzat!'

Umpire Dickie Bird responded with a panto-style shout of 'Oh no he isn't!'

Botham reckoned he got some of the worst reviews of any panto star. He appeared in *Babes in the Wood* and one critic wrote: 'Botham was more wooden than any tree in the forest.'

In the early days of mobile telephones, Dickie Bird was standing in the middle umpiring a match at Northampton when Allan Lamb came in to bat. He handed Dickie one of the newfangled phones and said, 'Meant to leave this in the dressing-room. Look after it for me, Dickie.'

Five minutes later the telephone rang, and Dickie jumped a foot in the air. Lamby, at the other end, shouted: 'Answer it, Dickie, and tell them to ring back.'

Dickie did as he was asked, and fumed when he found it was Botham on the line asking him the score.

Botham and Lamb were big pals throughout their Test careers. At a heavily liquid lunch to promote their 'Beefy and Lamby' advertising campaign in 2007, Allan was asked what was the cleanest story he could tell about sharing a room on tours with Beefy.

'Rooming with him was great,' he said. 'In three months I never saw him. That's probably the cleanest story.'

Botham added: 'Sleep is overrated. We had a great philosophy, Lamby and I. Playing with Geoffrey Boycott, we came to the conclusion that if he was not out overnight we didn't have to get home till five in the morning because he'd be out there all day tomorrow.'

What I like about Botham is that he puts his feet where his mouth is. He has walked more than seven thousand miles and raised over nine million quid for leukaemia charities. So he has talked the talk (now as an outstanding Sky cricket commentator), and has walked the walk. So it was only fitting that the Establishment at long last forgave him for some of the sillier things he got up to in his wilder days and awarded him the knighthood that he so richly deserved.

I reckon he should be given another award, though: in recognition of once draining six bottles of Rioja on a flight to Jamaica!

A cricketer who could match even Botham and Lamb as a prankster was former Hampshire skipper Colin Ingleby-Mackenzie, whose cavalier approach to the game (and life) is best summed up by his famous quote: 'I always insist that my players are in bed before ten o'clock during a match. After all, play starts at eleven-thirty!'

During his playing days with Yorkshire, Dickie Bird was shaping up to face a ball against Hampshire when he heard the sound of a horse-race commentary. He looked towards the slips to find Old Etonian Ingleby-Mackenzie with a transistor glued to his ear. 'Hope I'm not breaking your concentration, old chap,' said Ingers. 'I've got a few bob riding on a nag.'

Darren 'Dazzler' Gough is these days best known for his twinkling toes as the champion of *Strictly Come Dancing*, but he was first and foremost a great strike bowler for Yorkshire and England. He could knock the pints back as hard as he knocked the stumps over, and admitted that during one Test match against South Africa he went on to the pitch in an inebriated condition.

'I had drunk myself into such a state the night before that I was still feeling the effects as I arrived at the ground,' he recalled. 'I threw up in the dressing-room and I felt so bad I wasn't sure whether I had a hangover or was still drunk."

Nevertheless, he pulled himself together to play a key role in an England victory.

The England cricketers featured in this chapter are amateur guzzlers compared with some of the Aussies. David Boon established a new record (previously held by Rodney Marsh) when he downed fifty-two cans of lager on the flight from Sydney to London at the start of the 1989 Ashes tour. In recognition he became known as the 'Keg on Legs'.

The stockily built, mustachioed Boon was already a boozers' icon after vomiting on the Adelaide Oval turf the previous year in front of a TV audience of millions. He miraculously went on to make 122 runs and won the Man of the Match Award.

A drinking David Boon doll was created and given away in a beer promotion called 'Boonanza'. In Australia they don't ban boozing players; they lionise them!

Sir Garfield Sobers, whom even the likes of Botham and Flintoff would have to admit was the king of the all-rounders, had a theory that the later he stayed up on Test match days, the better he would perform. 'I liked to enjoy myself,' he said. 'That way I knew people were going to be critical and that would motivate me into showing just what I could do.'

Footballers find it harder than cricketers to be forgiven for their drunken exploits. It's probably to do with the shedloads of money they take home every week. I ask you, a hundred grand a week for kicking a lump of leather around a field! In my pub playing days I was happy to do it for an after-match pint or three.

Duncan Ferguson is perhaps the most notorious of all the recent footballing boozers, earning the unforgettable nickname 'Duncan Disorderly'. He got involved in three well-recorded brawls off the pitch, two of them taking place at taxi ranks and the other a fight with a fisherman in an Anstruther pub.

But it was an on-the-pitch altercation that brought him not only hurtful publicity but a prison sentence. He got three months for battering Jock McStay of Raith Rovers while playing for Rangers, prior to becoming a cult figure at Goodison.

Ferguson, a towering inferno of a player, tried to keep a low profile off the pitch once he transferred to Merseyside, but he was catapulted back on to the front pages when he interrupted two separate burglaries at his home. On each occasion the intruders had to have hospital treatment before being charged by the police.

He can hardly be called a gentle giant, but Duncan does have a soft, caring side, and I can vouch for the fact that he has done a lot of unpublicised charity work for the Alder Hey Children's Hospital in Liverpool. But he is probably at his happiest and calmest when pursuing his hobby of racing pigeons. Coo, fancy that.

'Jinky' Jimmy Johnstone was a winger with Jock Stein's Celtic, and Scots will tell you that he matched the likes of Matthews and Best as the greatest British winger of all time. And, just like Georgie, he used to make as many headlines off the pitch as on it with his eccentric and often drink-dictated behaviour.

He made Freddie Flintoff's pedalo adventure seem tame by comparison during preparations for a Home Championship match against England at Hampden Park. He and some high-spirited team-mates took a break from their coastal training camp and had a night on the town.

On the way back to the hotel Jinky jumped into a rowing boat. One of the other players gave it a push with his foot and it floated off into the darkness with the wee man – a non-swimmer – on board, standing up, singing 'Scotland the Brave'. Suddenly Jimmy realised not only that the boat did not have any oars but that it was leaking. It was caught in a current and on its way to the open sea when the coastguard came to his rescue.

Jimmy got a big bollocking from the Scottish FA, but they were not silly enough to drop him. He played a blinder the following Saturday to help Scotland sink England 2–0.

'Jinky' trailed the great midfield maestro Jim Baxter in the drinking league. 'Slim Jim' had prodigious skill but received only thirty-four Scottish caps. One thing's for sure, he could have drunk for Scotland, and he was continually involved in drunken nights while playing brilliant football for Rangers, Sunderland and Nottingham Forest. But he is best remembered for teasing and tormenting the World Cup-winning England team of the mid-1960s, sometimes playing keepy-uppy or sitting on the ball to prove that he was the master.

Shortly before his death from cancer in 2001, Jim was asked what he would have done with the huge wages paid to modern players. 'Och, it would have made no difference,' he said. 'I would have just spent more on drink and at the bookmaker's.'

Peter Osgood was an artist with the ball at his feet. Unfortunately, though, he also had a reputation for being a piss artist, which was why his exceptional ability was rewarded with only four caps during the Alf Ramsey/Don Revie era, when boozers were considered losers.

He was king of the pitch and in charge at the bar in the days when Chelsea had a hell of a drinking school, including Alan Hudson, Alan Birchenall and Charlie Cooke, all of whom could booze for Britain.

There appears to be something about the atmosphere at Chelsea – the nearest club to the bright lights of the West End – that breeds a boozing culture. John Terry was embroiled in several drunken brawls before he grew up and learned his responsibilities, while Dennis Wise was involved in an infamous wrecking of a taxi after leaving a club run by Terry Venables.

Back in the 1960s, Chelsea boss Tommy Docherty had to fine Osgood when he got legless the night before a League game. Ossie did not learn his lesson. Some time later, he and Alan Hudson staggered back to Stamford Bridge after a lunchtime drinking session and were fined by Dave Sexton, who had taken over from Docherty as manager.

Later, Dave took Osgood into his office, locked the door and offered to have things out man to man with his brilliant but undisciplined centre-forward. Ossie wisely declined the offer of a stand-up fight with a man who was the iron-hard son of former British middleweight contender Archie Sexton.

In spite of (or maybe because of) his reputation, Osgood became an idol at Stamford Bridge, a lovable rascal who could look as gifted as any footballer in the world.

He enjoyed his most famous drink-related adventure after moving to Southampton and helping them win the FA Cup in 1976, when they shocked Manchester United at Wembley.

Osgood had plenty of partying experience at Chelsea to call upon, and inevitably he was leading the celebrations when someone had the not so bright idea of giving him the Cup and telling him to get it back safely to Southampton. It was like putting a clown in charge of the Crown Jewels.

So it was that at three o'clock on the morning after the final a seriously sozzled Ossie was showing off the FA Cup to astonished Saints supporters having a coffee at a mobile snackbar on the A3. Then, as you do, Ossie took the Cup home and slept with it! 'It was the best way of looking after it and keeping it safe,' he later explained with the sort of logic that made sense only to him.

Sadly, they just don't have wonderful characters like Ossie in the game any more.

Talking of clowns, we now come to Gazza. Paul Gascoigne followed another North-East hero, Len Shackleton, as the Clown Prince of

Football, but the difference was that Gazza continued to play the clown *off* the pitch, more often than not with a glass in his hand.

I make no apologies for repeating a story that I often tell about my favourite goal of recent years, scored by Gazza while he was in the dog house over his drinking escapades. It came during the Euro 96 championships that were staged in England, and it deserves a full description, including the build-up to the match.

The England team managed by Terry Venables came into the tournament under a cloud of controversy after some of their drink-fuelled players had enjoyed a wild night out in Hong Kong following a match that had been scheduled as a warm-up for the action at home.

Gazza, who too often went a prank too far, as usual was at the centre of it all. He and several team-mates were photographed pouring drinks down each other's throats while lying in a pseudo dentist's chair in a nightclub. Then, on the flight home, several players were accused of causing damage to the aircraft. It was bad enough having fans as hooligans; now the players were behaving like louts!

Only an exceptional performance in the upcoming championships could restore their pride and self-respect. And that is exactly what they produced under the guidance of master-coach Venables.

England were held 1–1 by Switzerland in the opening game at Wembley, with a harsh penalty awarded against Stuart Pearce cancelling out an Alan Shearer goal and costing the home team a deserved victory.

Then came the 'British Final' – England against Scotland, who had held mighty Holland to a goalless draw in their first game. It was a cracker.

Trailing 1–0 to a Shearer goal, the Scots were awarded a penalty twelve minutes from the end. David Seaman saved superbly from Gary McAllister, and within a minute the one and only Gazza had scored a gem of a second for England. He cleverly and cheekily chipped the ball over the head of his Rangers club-mate Colin Hendry, collected it on its way down and found the net with an exquisite shot. It was a goal in the Pelé class.

'Daft-as-a-brush' Gazza – former England manager Bobby Robson's nickname for him – celebrated by going to a chosen spot at the side of the Scottish goal, and as he lay down England team-mates poured bottled water down his throat in a non-alcoholic send-up of the dentist's chair incident. The crowd loved it, and suddenly the England players were forgiven their boisterous behaviour in the Far East.

Unfortunately, it was all downhill from there for Gazza. He continued to hit the bottle and was in and out of rehab like a drunk in a revolving door. But he remains one of the best-loved sporting characters in the country, and everybody is hoping he will finally beat the booze for good. The pictures we prefer in our memories are not of a legless Gazza but of him playing out of his skin in the 1990 World Cup or commanding the pitch at Wembley in Euro 96.

One thing's for sure – as the chant goes – 'There's only one Paul Gascoigne.'

Gazza should choose Tony Adams as his role model. The former Arsenal and England centre-half and now Portsmouth assistant manager has proved you can beat the bottle with one-day-at-a-time iron will and discipline.

At the peak (or should I say depths) of his drinking he served time as a guest at one of Her Majesty's establishments, and while drunk at the wheel of his car smashed into a wall. The joke that whirled around at the time was that he was trying to get the wall back ten yards.

His ex-Arsenal team-mate Paul Merson had a triple whammy, not only a drink problem but drugs and gambling addictions that saw him go through thousands of pounds and eventually fall into bankruptcy. The lasting image he left with Arsenal fans was making tilted-glass gestures with both hands to supporters while celebrating a cup victory in 1994.

Merson is one of many whom Tony Adams has tried to help with his Sporting Chance Clinic, which was set up with the aim of putting sportsmen who have hit troubled times on the road to recovery.

A drinking culture in football is nothing new. Irish international defender Paul McGrath admitted to alcohol problems while playing for Manchester United. He said: 'I used to drink to give myself Dutch courage.'

That smooth-as-silk player Stan Bowles was ahead of Paul Merson, with the double-headed monster of gambling and drinking problems. He revealed that when he appeared on the BBC TV show *Superstars*, he had been up until the early hours the night before smoking cigars and drinking pints of lager, glasses of wine and large brandies.

On the day of the show, his athletic efforts resulted in just seven points – the lowest score in the history of the programme!

It was unfortunate for Bradford City captain Stuart McCall that cameras were trained on him as he celebrated the promotion of the Bantams to the Premiership. Lager in hand, he decided to leap on to the top of a car and dance. Big mistake.

He went arse over tit off the roof of the car, yet somehow came up smiling. The watching fans roared their appreciation. He had not spilled a drop of his lager!

Just for laughs, I have compiled the following countdown of British foot-ballers behaving badly (and sometimes madly):

10 Jermaine Pennant (2005)
During his days with Arsenal, the then twenty-two-year-old midfielder was given a three-month prison sentence after admitting drink-driving while disqualified and having no insurance. When stopped, he was dragging a wrecked lamppost behind his car, and he gave a false name in what the police described as a slurred voice. He was released from

prison after a month and played for Birmingham while wearing an electronic tag.

After reviving his career with a successful move to Anfield, defenders didn't find it so easy to tag him.

9 Alan Shearer (1997)

According to David Batty's well-publicised autobiography, Newcastle's players went out on the piss during a break in Dublin in 1997. It developed into one of those silly nights and Belgian defender Philippe Albert ended up walking around with a traffic cone on his head. As they became increasingly inebriated, Northern Ireland international Keith Gillespie started flicking bottle tops at Shearer, who warned him if he didn't stop he would get a good hiding. The two team-mates went outside and suddenly the other players looked out of the window to see a pair of legs going up in the air.

'We ran out,' Batty recorded, 'and saw Gillespie spark out in the gutter. There was blood everywhere. Keith had apparently taken the first swing and Al just turned and decked him.'

The usually spotless Shearer was called the 'Mary Poppins of football' by Newcastle chairman Freddy Shepherd. I wonder if he offered Gillespie a spoonful of sugar after he had dished out the medicine?

8 Jody Morris (2001)

This is another example of the Chelsea drinking culture. On the day after the 9/11 attacks grieving Americans complained to the management of a Heathrow hotel that a group of footballers were making drunken pests of themselves. Newspapers were tipped off and several Chelsea players including twenty-two-year-old Jody Morris were named and shamed.

It was inevitable that Jody was involved. After a binge in Wimbledon the previous year he had spent the night in a police cell for being drunk and disorderly. He was reported to the police for brawling in a pub, and a month after the Heathrow incident he was involved in a nightclub fight. There's obviously something in the water at Chelsea (probably Scotch).

7 Peter Shilton (1980)

England's most capped player, with 125 internationals under his belt, lost his usual poise when he was startled by a man banging on his car window in the middle of the night while he was parked in a country lane. The trouble was the man was the none-too-chuffed husband of the woman who was sharing the car with England's finest. Shilts sped off, but in his panic he crashed into a lamppost (I'm not sure if it was the near or the far post). Before long, the police arrived and charged him with drink-driving. In court he gallantly admitted 'taking a lady for a meal' and was fined £350 and banned from driving for fifteen months. He also had to endure teasing terrace chants of 'Shilton, Shilton, where's your wife?' for years afterwards.

6 Don Hutchison (1996)

The tabloids were sent photographic proof that Liverpool's Scottish international had dropped his trousers and stuck a Budweiser label on his manhood while on a holiday drinking spree in Cyprus. When his boss at Anfield, Roy Evans, was told of the incident he allegedly sighed: 'If he's been showing it again, that's out of order.'

A year earlier, it was reliably reported that Hutchison had unzipped in a bar where some girl students were videoing each other and said: 'Zoom in on this!'

After the flash in Cyprus he was fined five thousand quid, dropped, transfer-listed and eventually sold to West Ham, where, of course, the fans nicknamed him 'Budweiser'.

5 Stan Collymore (2000)

Leicester City's players were taking a four-day break in La Manga before the Worthington Cup final. On the first night after some heavy drinking by the squad, Stan Collymore let off a fire extinguisher in the hotel's piano bar. The team was sent packing back to Leicester, but they returned to Spain four years later, only to have three players end up in the sex offenders' wing at Murcia Jail. All allegations against the trio were later dropped.

4 Dwight Yorke (1998)

Well known for scoring off as well as on the pitch, Manchester United striker Dwight Yorke secretly taped a booze-driven sex romp involving himself, Aston Villa's goalkeeper Mark Bosnich and four girls at his luxury house in Sutton Coldfield. The video showed Yorke and Bosnich giving thumbs-ups to the secret camera and wearing women's clothing! Somehow a tabloid newspaper got its hands on the film, and Old Trafford manager Alex Ferguson gave Yorke the famous hairdryer treatment for *dragging* United into the scandal.

3 Billy Bremner (1975)

Scotland had beaten Denmark 0–1 in Copenhagen and skipper Billy Bremner led Willie Young, Joe Harper, Joe McCluskey and Arthur Graham in celebrations at a nightclub. The problem was that they were supposed to have been tucked up in bed in their hotel. They got totally bladdered in the club, and police were called after Bremner had been accused of throwing a beer over a barmaid. The police found themselves having to battle with five drunken Scots, and McCluskey removed a shoe and tried to use it as an offensive weapon. They were finally kicked back to their hotel, where they wrecked the room of one of the Scottish Football Association officials. All five were subsequently banned for life from playing for Scotland.

2 Mickey Thomas (1993)

Nicknamed the 'Welsh George Best', Mickey Thomas admitted that when playing for Manchester United and Chelsea he used to sit up drinking into the early hours on match days to conquer his nerves. In 1993 he was jailed for eighteen months for passing fake ten- and twenty-pound notes. Now a very funny after-dinner speaker, he cracks: 'I was well ahead of today's players in being on fifty grand a week. Mind you, it all ended when police found my printing machine.'

1 Peter Beagrie (1991)

This one had us roaring with laughter on Merseyside. Everton were on a pre-season tour of Spain, and Beagrie went out on the razzle following a game with Real Sociedad. It was the early hours of the morning when he arrived back at the team hotel on the back of a motorcycle driven by a friendly Spaniard. Despite banging on the hotel's locked front door, he couldn't rouse the night porter. So with true drunken logic, he grabbed the bike, rode it up the hotel steps and went straight through a plate-glass window.

At least he got in. The trouble was, it was the wrong hotel!

Beagrie was taken off to hospital and needed fifty stitches for his lacerations.

Why is it that when Rugby Union players get involved in drinking sprees it is known as high-jinks, but when it involves footballers it's hooliganism?

The funniest drink-dominated story I've heard from the international rugby circuit goes back to the 1980s, before the game turned professional and the players had to be more responsible.

During the official banquet following a France–England game in Paris, the two teams decided to indulge in a little drinking competition.

England's mischievous forward Maurice Colclough had earlier emptied the contents of his gift bottle of after-shave into an ice-bucket and replaced it with water. He downed the contents of the bottle in one, watched in impressed amazement by his team-mates and the French. Not wishing to be outdone, Colclough's fellow-pack member Colin Smart unscrewed the top of his own bottle of aftershave and drank it down.

Not-so-Smart ended up in hospital having his stomach pumped, prompting the England scrum-half Steve Smith to observe sympathetically, 'Colin was in a bad way, but his breath smelled lovely!'

From then on, the prop was known as Colin 'The Brut' Smart.

Chris Finnegan set something of a record after winning the boxing middleweight gold medal at the 1968 Olympics in Mexico. He was so dehydrated after the fight that it took six hours and ten pints of beer before he could produce a urine sample to prove he was 'clean'.

'I finished up with two Olympic officials leaving the stadium with me and coming to a restaurant where we had a celebration meal,' he recalled. 'We were about an hour into the meal when I suddenly stood up and said, "Right, who wants some piss!"'

The most delirious drinking ever witnessed at a sporting event on television was surely that which followed Europe's Ryder Cup victory over the United States in 2006.

Leading the way was skipper Ian Woosnam, holding a magnum of champagne that seemed almost as big as the man himself. He was caught unawares as the bubbly erupted, covering him in champers, but it didn't stop him trying to drain the bottle.

Then man-of-the-moment Darren Clarke took just seven seconds to sink a pint of Guinness.

Woosie was by now on the black stuff too, and he managed to get it down him (on his shirt as well as in his mouth) as he tried to match the speed of Clarke. He was just moments away from having to deliver his captain's speech, and you wondered how he was going to manage to stand up, let alone get out any gracious words. But he pulled himself together sufficiently to muster a few sentences, before returning to a long night of liquid celebrations.

Max Faulkner, the colourful 1951 Open champion, employed a regular caddie nicknamed 'Mad Mac', who was, to say the least, a bit eccentric. He wore a raincoat but no shirt, and he always studied the greens through binoculars from which the lenses had been removed.

Faulkner was teeing off in a domestic tournament when he noticed his caddie swaying as if in a strong wind. 'Are you all right?' asked Max.

'I'm as trim as a daisy,' replied Mac in a slurred voice. 'I've just polished off a bottle of brandy, and I'll start on another one when you've won this tournament.'

Faulkner birdied the hole, then looked around for Mac. The caddie was flat out by the side of the green with the flag clasped in his arms.

Max replaced the flag in the hole himself, then half carried and half dragged Mac behind a gorse bush, where he left him sleeping like a baby.

Snooker seems to be a magnet for mavericks, and you could fill a book with the drink and drug exploits of a procession of players.

There was one man who outdrank (and outsmoked) them all – big Bill Werbeniuk, who used to weigh in at twenty stone, and it was nothing for him to drain ten pints during a match. He also chain-smoked while waiting for his turn at the table.

Canadian Bill was quite a character. During one occasion at the Crucible he loudly broke wind as he bent over to play a shot. He stepped back and stared into the crowd. 'OK, own up,' he said. 'Who did that?'

Werbeniuk got a medical certificate to prove that he had to take the drug Inderal while playing, and he mixed this with the drink and cigarettes. He also claimed tax relief on his booze intake because he said it was essential to counteract an inherited arm tremor.

Following his last professional match in 1990 he revealed: 'I've had twenty-four pints of extra-strong lager and eight double vodkas and I'm still not drunk.'

He lost the match 10–1. I wonder how many balls he was seeing?

You've gotta laugh

Three men are sitting at the bar comparing Edinburgh pubs. One says: 'Aye, this is a nice bar, but there's a better one. At McAllister's, you buy a drink, you buy another drink, and then McAllister himself will buy your third drink!'

The second man responds: 'Och, that's nothing compared with McCormick's. He's such a good publican that he buys every other drink.'

'You think that's generous?' pipes up the third man. 'There's a pub across town called Armstrong's. They buy you your first drink, they buy you your second drink, they buy your third drink, and then they take you in the back and get you laid!'

'Wow!' chorus the other two. 'That sounds fantastic! Did that actually happen to you?'

'No,' replies their friend, 'but it happened to my sister!'

Hark Who's Talking About Drink

'Alcohol is the anaesthesia by which we endure the operation of life.'
– George Bernard Shaw

'In victory, you deserve champagne. In defeat, you need it.'
– Napoleon Bonaparte

'When you stop drinking, you suddenly have to deal with this personality that started you drinking in the first place.'
– Jimmy Breslin

'I have to think very hard of an interesting man who does not drink.'
– Richard Burton

'My doctor has told me it's dangerous to keep drinking a bottle of Scotch a day, so now I only drink it at night.'
– Tommy Cooper

'The best research for playing a drunk is being a British actor for twenty years.'
– Michael Caine

'If you resolve to give up smoking, drinking and loving, you don't actually live longer; it just seems longer.'
– Clement Freud

'Alcohol brings a temporary relief to a problem. Enjoy that brief moment. It could be the best thing that happens to you.'
– Charles Coburn

'The greatest question in the English language: "What are you having?"'
– John Edwards

'I have reached that stage in my life when I am more concerned about the hangover I'm going to have than the beer I am going to drink.'
– Fred Emney

'I cannot remember if my wife left me because of my drinking, or I started drinking because she left me.'
– Nicolas Cage

'I am keeping a promise to my wife, and this will be the last glass of beer I ever drink. In future I shall drink straight from the bottle.'
– Ted Rogers

9 ▶ Fly Me to the Moon

If you have read my award-winning novel *Searching for the Rock Island Line* (end of commercial), you will know I was in at the ground floor of the rock 'n' roll revolution that rocked and shocked the world. Mind you, I went for the soft option of skiffle while a few Liverpool streets away the Beatles were just starting out on their way to fame and fortune.

When they went to Hamburg to lay the foundation to their legend, I stayed behind in Liverpool strumming on my banjo under the name of Hobo Rick and with a trio called the Hi-Fi Three. OK, we didn't become quite as famous as John and Paul, but I bet we had just as much fun.

We concentrated as much on comedy as music, including mad, off-the-wall sketches long before *Monty Python* slithered on to our television sets. Much of it was surreal, drink-fuelled fun in the springtime of my life when I could sink a pint without it touching the sides of my throat.

I worked as a plasterer during the week, then got plastered at the weekends when, as Hobo Rick, I used to play at heavy-duty drinking places like the Mediterranean, Ozzie Wade's, the Blue House at Stanley Park Hotel, the Bow and Arrow and the notorious Colombo Club in Seel Street, where there were more crooks and gangsters than in the old Walton Prison.

One of the most popular parts of our ad-libbed comedy shows

Here's to memories of Hobo Rick and the Hi-Fi Three. Cheers my arse!

was a sort of *X-Factor* singing competition, but we were looking for the *worst* warbler rather than the best. So it was more of a *Why?-Factor*. The winner would get something like an old wellington boot or a kettle that no longer whistled. As we were all three-quarters boozed it didn't matter, as long as we had a laugh.

You have to remember that this was in the days of clubs trying to find ways around the crazy licensing laws, so that they could serve drinks after the pubs had closed.

During one of our 'talent shows' – and I use the phrase in its loosest form – I noticed a fella trying to jump the queue of performers who were waiting to take the stage. 'Oi, wait your turn,' I said, but he wouldn't listen and kept pushing his way through the throng.

'All right then,' I said, 'I can see you're not taking "no" for an answer.'

I gave him a friendly clip around the back of the head as he clambered up on stage. 'A little hush, please,' I announced. 'Give a bit of order for this dopey twat, who's insisting on giving us a song.'

I looked at him and asked, 'What's it going to be, pal?'

He took the microphone from me and revealed: 'My name is Detective Inspector Coffee and this is a police raid.'

Six uniformed coppers with clipboards under their arms came marching through the main door and down between the tables. Everybody there was going to be charged with illegal drinking.

Well, I say 'everybody'. Within seconds of the words 'police raid' being uttered, one hundred people vanished into the night, scrambling down a fire escape at the side of the club. A keen young copper raised his hand and shouted, 'Stop! Police.' I think he might still be picking himself up after being trampled in the stampede. He probably ended up literally as a bent copper.

It finished with the six policemen and Inspector Coffee having a drink at the empty bar with Rick Hobo and the rest of the Hi-Fi Three.

A few years later, I applied for a licence to run a banjo parlour in the Liverpool Docks area, and when I called into the office, who was doing the interviewing but Inspector Coffee! I recognised him in an instant (sorry!) and couldn't resist asking why it had taken so long for the police to raid the Colombo.

'We had it under surveillance for years,' he told me, 'but we decided to leave be because at least we knew where all the villains were! The only reason we raided it when we did was because other legally run clubs were complaining that the Colombo was nicking all their custom.'

Copyright © Richard Young/Rex Features

Keith Moon, who could beat the drums but not the bottle. There was a dark side to the Moon.

My rock 'n' roll years might have been lubricated by a beer or three, but I don't think I was in quite the same league as the mad master of wrecking-while-rocking, the Who's wild drummer Keith Moon.

Let's begin with his infamous twenty-first birthday party at the Holiday Inn in Flint, Michigan, in 1967. He started it in some style by driving a Cadillac into the hotel's swimming pool. To stop the police arresting the birthday boy, the band's co-manager Chris Stamp paid the sheriff fifty thousand dollars on the spot.

But Keith was far from finished for the night. He moved on to a room hired by Peter Noone of Herman's Hermits (they knocked around together and were known as Moon and Noone, the Loon Twins). A huge birthday cake was brought in, but instead of cutting it in the conventional way Moon and Noone decided to have a food fight, using it as ammunition. Soon everybody was down to their underpants and hurling cake across the crowded room.

Moon clambered up on to a table to get a better shot but was so paralytic that he tumbled face first to the floor and broke his two front teeth. He was carted off to the local hospital but they refused to help him because he was so full of alcohol. Eventually Herman's Hermits lent their tour helicopter so that Keith could be transported to an emergency dentist.

Here's something I bet you didn't know. In that same year, when the Beatles did their historic first global satellite link-up during the recording of 'All You Need Is Love', Moon the Loon was in the background singing harmonies with Mick Jagger, Eric Clapton, Graham Nash and a crowd of other rockers.

In the same month, he destroyed his drum kit (literally: he blew it up) in a ferocious climax to the Who's performance at the Monterey Pop Festival. Peaceful and loving California had never seen anything like it.

Back in London in November 1968 Keith was fined two pounds – yes, just two quid – for being drunk and disorderly in the West End. 'Now, we don't want you playing in traffic any more,' the paternal magistrate warned him.

'Absolutely, old chap,' replied Keith (who spoke with an exaggerated posh accent). 'They already have a drummer.' No doubt the magistrate was completely mystified by Keith's reference to Steve Winwood's band.

A week before the Who triumphed at Woodstock in 1969, Moon made a guest appearance with the insane Bonzo Dog Doo-Dah Band. He decided to appear incognito, wearing a mask and calling himself the Loan Arranger. He staggered on from stage left carrying three pints of beer, one of which he managed to pour over Bonzo Dog's tap-dancing drummer 'Legs' Smith.

Meanwhile, the band's singer Viv Stanshall, in the Moon mould for lunacy, used to be his straight man in a gag they played in clothing stores. They would ask the assistant to bring them the strongest pair of trousers in the shop.

They would then take a leg each as if testing the strength, and tear them apart. As the shocked staff looked on, wondering what they could do with a pair of ruined trousers, a one-legged friend of theirs would come hopping in and say, 'Just what I've been looking for. Wonderful!'

Keith threw a party in his hotel suite in Charlotte, North Carolina, in 1971, and decided that the television was too loud. Instead of turning it down, he pulled it from the wall – socket and all – and hurled it out of the window. His room was eight storeys up. The night porter came rushing to the room, and Moon, in his best English accent, apologised profusely for the 'sheer accident', gave him a bundle of dollars, then said: 'Oh, and by the way, when you get a spare second bring us a couple more bottles of chilled champers, there's a good chap.'

The porter was just about to exit when Keith added: 'Oh yes, my man, and one more thing. Can you rustle up another TV set?'

His favourite party trick was to let off 'cherry bombs' – explosives that he used to blow up his drum kit on stage – in hotel toilets, and tell the staff it was down to a bad curry he'd had in their restaurant.

Unsurprisingly, he was banned and evicted from hotels and motels worldwide. Another jape was putting an inflatable doll into a bath of water, then calling down to reception to report in a panic-stricken voice that there was a dead body in his bathroom.

Everything Moon the Loon did was designed to make people laugh. 'There are too many miserable f****** in this world,' he used to say. He would turn up at functions dressed as the Queen, Hitler, a circus clown or anybody else he thought might have a shock effect.

One of his albums was called *All This and World War II*, and to get in the mood he went to the studio dressed as the Desert Fox, Field Marshal Rommel. After some recording, he got into a drinking binge with two other Premier League boozers, Harry Nilsson and Joe Cocker, and by the end he was so drunk that he collapsed on the beach outside his LA home. His next-door neighbour, amazingly enough, was Steve McQueen, and early the next morning Steve's son told his dad in a panic that there was a dead Nazi on the beach. Steve ran out to find Moon, still in his Rommel uniform, sleeping like a baby with the ocean lapping at his feet.

Moon spent money like there was no tomorrow. Among his more eccentric purchases were a pink Rolls-Royce and – in startling contrast – an electric-powered milk float. He had the latter converted into what he called his 'mobile Victorian parlour', complete with armchair, wallpaper, cocktail cabinet and gramophone. To fit it into his garage, he decided he needed to relocate his Corvette. But where to put it? Unable to think of an answer, he simply drove it into a nearby hedge.

Because his madness and eccentricity – fuelled by drink and pills – overshadowed everything else, we tend to forget that Keith was one of the greatest rock 'n' roll drummers of all time. He could really play those skins, attacking them with a ferocity that gave the Who an atomic beat . . . and you can often hear him on their records yelling in accompaniment to his drum solos.

But nobody can live life in the fast lane twenty-four hours a day, and he was soon burned out. Before long, he was paying the price for doing such crazy things as downing twenty Margaritas to win a bet, picking up Oliver Reed in his helicopter and the pair of them drinking the nearest pub dry, and popping uppers and downers like Smarties.

Keith was found dead from an accidental overdose of prescription drugs in a Mayfair apartment owned by Harry Nilsson on 7 September 1978. Chillingly, he passed on in the very room where Mama Cass (of the Mamas and the Papas) had died of a heart attack four years earlier.

Like Keith, Mama Cass had been just thirty-two. Like a mad cat, Moon the Loon had gone through nine lives in (a sadly short) one.

A big shock was that Joe Cocker lived to see the new millennium. And Joe himself was more surprised than anyone. In fact, as the old joke goes, I'm sure if Joe had known he was going to live so long he would have taken better care of himself. He was in the Keith Moon class for mixing alcohol and drugs into a dangerous cocktail.

Cocker, the man with a voice like rusty made-in-Sheffield razorblades, gave an insight into what he called 'the lost years' in interviews while plugging his 2007 album *Hymn for My Soul*. They often say that if you can remember the sixties, you weren't there. But it was the next decade that did most damage to Joe's memory.

Joe Cocker has somehow survived, with a little help from his friends.

'The seventies are just a blur to me,' he admitted. 'I was so out of it that I could hardly even remember the words to my own hit songs. I was living on a liquid diet. My routine was to start drinking as soon as I got out of bed in the morning, sometimes starting while still in bed. By the evening I was pretty wasted and used to go on stage with everything a blur. People used to tell me as I came off at the end that I had been great. I used to get so carried away that I would physically damage myself by the end of each gig. They were crazy days, what I can remember of them.'

In October 1972, Cocker toured Australia with his Mad Dogs and Englishmen entourage, and there was a mass brawl at the Commodore Chateau in Melbourne after six of the group were arrested for possessing drugs. It all came to a head with Joe being

172

given forty-eight hours to leave the country by the Australian Federal Police.

In America, the Mad Dogs tour played in forty-eight cities in fifty-six days. No wonder Joe finished up in hospital suffering from severe exhaustion.

In 1976, John Belushi, who could teach even Cocker a thing or three about mixing drugs and alcohol, joined him on stage in a parody of his hit 'With a Little Help from My Friends' for the hugely popular *Saturday Night Live* TV show. The Bible Belt erupted with criticism of the 'I'll get high with a little help from my friends' line, during which Belushi and Cocker mimed taking drugs and pouring beer over themselves.

This performance inspired the idea for *The Blues Brothers*, the film in which Belushi and Dan Aykroyd became cult heroes before John's tragic, drug-related death in 1982.

The annual Brit Awards is always sure to feature rock 'n' rollers behaving badly. I'm not sure booze was to blame for the biggest debacle, when former Page 3 model Samantha Fox was paired with Fleetwood Mac's Mick Fleetwood in the greatest (if unintended) comedy pairing since Laurel and Hardy. But their performance certainly must have driven the producers to drink.

It all got off to a good start when tiny Sam went to giant Mick's microphone, and he crouched to try to talk into hers. It was like something out of *Monty Python*. From thereon, they continually fluffed their lines, guests arrived late and often seemed to be in another world, and a pre-recorded message from Michael Jackson went missing, so a Bros video was hastily tacked on at the end to stop the show finishing early.

One of the most memorable moments came when Fox and Fleetwood talked over each other while introducing the Four Tops, only for Boy George to walk out on stage. 'I'm afraid I'm just the one Top,' said a bemused George.

Another Brit Awards highlight was when Michael Jackson was mock-mooned on stage by Pulp singer Jarvis Cocker in a protest against Wacko's pretentiousness. Yes, cheers my arse!

Robbie Williams used one of his acceptance speeches at the Brits to offer to fight Liam Gallagher for a £100,000 side-stake. Gallagher did not need any lessons from Williams in how to be a young man behaving badly at the event. At a previous show he had mimed sticking his award where the sun don't shine after telling guest presenter Michael Hutchence: 'Has-beens shouldn't be presenting awards to gonna-bes.'

They keep trying to give the Brits extra clout by inviting along politicians, even though it always ends in disaster. At least Prime Minister Margaret Thatcher was crossed off the wanted list when she revealed that her favourite song was 'How Much Is That Doggy in the Window?', but plenty of others have shown up and regretted it. John Prescott got an ice bucket tipped over him by anarchist rocker Danbert Nobacon, and Elton John expressed his disgust when his 'Outstanding Contribution to Music' award was presented by the Conservative Party Chairman Norman Tebbit, who was anything but an advocate of gay rights.

Little-known DJ Brandon Block was the centre of controversy in 2000 after appearing uninvited on stage, expecting an award. Friends had managed to convince the heavily intoxicated Block that his name had just been announced and up he went, to their great amusement and his acute embarrassment.

Rolling Stones guitarist Ronnie Wood, who was about to present the award to the genuine recipient, aimed an insult at Block, who retaliated, so Wood threw a drink over him. What a waste of a good pint!

No collection of rock 'n' roll stories would be complete without a few more contributions from the Rolling Stones, who seem to have been around longer than Mars bars.

Their most controversial moments have been drug rather than alcohol related, but they have put away gallons of booze in their time. During a drunken party in Toronto's Harbour Castle Hotel in 1977, fifteen Royal Canadian Mounted Police made a raid and arrested guitarist Keith Richards for being in possession of heroin. If found guilty, he faced a minimum seven-year prison sentence. However, it was all slightly embarrassing for the Canadians because among the party-goers was their Prime Minister's wife, Margaret Trudeau.

A blind woman got Richards (and the Canadian Establishment) off the hook. She approached the trial judge and told him that the often-stoned Stone had gone out of his way to arrange rides for her to the group's concerts and free tickets. The judge was so impressed that he let Richards off with a one-year suspended sentence and the order to play two benefit concerts for the blind.

'I couldn't believe it,' a relieved Richards said. 'I had said good-bye to the band, my friends and family because I was convinced I was going down for seven years. To get caught like I was and then get off with playing a couple of concerts for the blind. That's got to be one for the *Guinness Book of Records*.'

When Richards made a cameo appearance in a *Pirates of the Caribbean* film (as Johnny Depp's father), cast member Bill Nighy said that he was so drunk that the director had to hold his shins to stop him falling over during the takes.

Keith gave a whole new meaning to 'being out of his tree' when he injured himself falling out of a coconut tree while on holiday in Fiji. At first it seemed he might have suffered brain damage; thankfully that turned out not to be the case. But a few months later it looked like he was still not totally compos mentis when it was reported that he had confessed to snorting his father's ashes. Everyone who knew him well was convinced he had said it as a typically self-deprecating joke, but a reporter had taken it seriously and flashed the story around the world.

Keith could always be counted on for a quote to remember. During one tour in the eighties he said at a press conference: 'It's good to be here . . . It's good to be anywhere . . . Where are we?'

In 1970 Mick Jagger said: 'I'd rather be dead than singing "Satisfaction" when I'm forty-five.' In December 2003, aged sixty, he became 'Sir Mick' and he was still singing 'Satisfaction'. Was this the same rebellious Jagger who in 1965 was fined along with Bill Wyman and Brian Jones for taking a piss in public? He joined Sir Elton John and Sir Paul McCartney as rock 'n' roll knights. Whatever happened to those wild boys who were out to shock the Establishment?

Charlie Watts, the jazz-oriented drummer who gives the Stones their drive, has always known his value to the group. He once told Jagger: 'Don't you call me your f****** drummer, *you're* my f****** singer.'

There were many of us on Merseyside in the 1960s astonished by the success of the Beatles. All wearing the same arse-hugging velvet-collar suits, and those stupid mop-top hairstyles. Let's be honest, it was hardly cool. I didn't rate them in the top five bands in Liverpool, let alone in the world. Ahead of them, in my opinion, were Ian and the Zodiacs, Derry and the Seniors, Rory Storm and the Hurricanes and the Big Three. But, as we all know, it was the Beatles who made it, so maybe I'm not a good judge.

Much better than accepting knighthoods, I preferred the Beatles story that circulated when they were awarded MBEs back in 1965. They apparently shared a joint in the Buckingham Palace cloakroom before the ceremony. Now *that's* rock 'n' roll!

I like to think that, had he lived, John Lennon would have stayed true to his roots and turned down the offer of a knighthood. It was John who returned his MBE in 1969 wrapped in brown paper as a protest at British involvement in Biafra and America's war in Vietnam.

David Bowie refused to sell out and turned down a knighthood in 2003. I'm sure he remembers doing that, but he freely admits he does not recall much of the 1970s. 'For instance,' he says, '1975 is a total blank. I cannot remember a thing about it. That's what drugs can do to you. I have to read the words of my own hit songs on stage, otherwise I could mess up while everybody listening knows exactly what comes next.'

Sir Elton John has survived huge drinking and drug-taking binges. And he gave a whole new meaning to 'flower power' when it emerged during a contract battle that he spent £293,000 on flowers between January 1996 and September 1997. Questioned by a barrister as to why he had spent so much, Elton had the court rocking with laughter when he answered simply: 'I like flowers.'

He used to like a drink too, but he has shown tremendous character and willpower by being dry for yonks

Elvis Presley loved a drink, but usually had it under control. His major problem was with prescription drugs: uppers and downers that made him lurch from feeling happily high or desperately low. And it was gluttony that hurried his death at the age of forty-two in 1977.

A little over a year before he died, two policemen from Colorado got into conversation with Elvis while visiting his Graceland home. They told a story that captured his gargantuan appetite.

Elvis mentioned a sandwich that he had once eaten at the Colorado Gold Mine Company restaurant in Denver: a hollowed-out, buttered loaf, filled with peanut butter, grape jelly and a pound of fried bacon. The sandwich was meant to feed eight, but Presley claimed that he had finished one himself.

The policemen were incredulous. Sensing their disbelief, Elvis insisted they should head to Denver – a distance of a thousand miles – so that he could prove he was not exaggerating.

He summoned his stretch Mercedes that whisked them to Memphis airport, where his private jet, the *Lisa Marie* – 'tastefully' upholstered in plush aquamarine leather – awaited. Two hours later, they landed in

Denver. Twenty-two of the $49.95 'Fool's Gold' sandwiches on silver platters, plus a bucket of Perrier water and a case of champagne, were brought to a private hangar at the airport by the Gold Mine Company restaurateur, his wife and a waiter.

Elvis proceeded to out-eat the two policemen, who were no doubt all shook up by the King's appetite. No wonder he was busting out of his jumpsuits in his final years.

Although not an alcoholic himself, Elvis managed to turn a close 'friend' into one. He owned a chimp named Scatter, who ate at the dinner table with a knife and fork and was chauffeured around in a Rolls-Royce. One of the 'tricks' Elvis taught Scatter was how to drink bourbon. The poor chimp died a premature death from cirrhosis of the liver, possibly the first in history to suffer that fate.

Just to encourage debate, here is a countdown of British rock 'n' rollers behaving badly (and sometimes madly) . . .

10 Rod Stewart Booze, blonde birds and football . . . Rod Stewart had it all to overflowing in his early days with the Faces before relaunching himself as one of the world's biggest solo stars. He really lived the rock 'n' roll dream before settling down to married life (three times) and fathering seven kids.

Rod has a 'lived-in' voice that moved Chuck Berry to say: 'This is a white guy singing? You've gotta be kidding me!'

'He's the greatest of all white soul singers,' said his old rival Elton John, who at one time seemed to be having a competition with Stewart to see who could sink the most booze.

Rod learned early on about the dangers of mixing drugs and alcohol. He had a good drink before going on stage to ease the nerves, but then an older member of the band gave him a Black Bomber, a powerful amphetamine. Big mistake! He was pushed off stage after singing the same song for twenty minutes and the same verse over and over again like a stuck record.

His hard rocker image took a dent when his former blonde squeeze Britt Ekland revealed to the world that he often wore her cotton panties on stage. 'He wore my knickers and pulled them up real tight and stuck the teeny-weeny part up his bum, so that he did not have any panty lines. It gave him the perfect rear end, and no one wiggled it quite like Rod.'

Cheers My Arse!

9 Robbie Williams Since leaving Take That to start his incredibly successful solo career, Robbie Williams has sold more than fifty million albums worldwide. He is worth an estimated £110 million, has bedded some of the world's most beautiful ladies, and is the bestselling recording artist outside North America. But is he happy?

He admits to being a manic depressive, and has tried booze (gallons of it) and pills to alleviate the black moods, but he is only really content when on stage performing in front of his thousands of dedicated fans.

When he signed a recording contract worth eighty million quid he shouted with a wild grin: 'I'm rich beyond my wildest dreams.' But I'm sure he'd rather be happy beyond his wildest dreams.

My favourite Robbie story occurred at a celebrity-packed party. 'I was completely and totally off my face,' he recalled. 'I stood staring at this painting for ages, almost hypnotised by it.

'U2's Bono came up to me and asked, "What are you doing, Robbie?" I said, "Bono, man, just take a look at this."

'He said: "Look at what?"

'"This painting," I said. "It's f****** fantastic."

'"Robbie," he said. "I don't want to disappoint you, but that's a window."'

8 Ronnie Wood Out of the same hard-drinking school as Rod Stewart, Ronnie Wood is our representative of the Rolling Stones in this top ten. He makes it in ahead of Keith Richards because of his legendary alcohol intake.

Ronnie is an accomplished artist (painting, that is, not piss) as well as one of the great rock guitarists, and the limited editions of his works are much sought after. His striking painting of Jack Nicholson hangs in the Hollywood actor's home.

He has achieved all this while fighting alcoholism for much of his life.

Ronnie wears a medallion that reads: 'God grant me the serenity to accept the things I cannot change, the courage to change the things I can, and the wisdom to know the difference.' He says that it helps him take one day at a time.

The true story I've dug up about Ronnie has nothing to do with rock 'n' roll, but it is so unbelievable that I had to include it here.

In 1996 his long-time pal, snooker ace Jimmy White, invited Ronnie to take part in a little tribute to Jimmy's brother, Martin, who had just died from cancer at the age of fifty-two. Jimmy wanted him to have one more night out on the town.

'Jimmy and some mates got Martin out of the morgue,' recalled Ronnie, 'dressed him in his best clobber and then there was this big party, with Martin as the guest of honour.

'"It's what Martin would have wanted," said Jimmy. "It was a chance to say a proper goodbye."'

Ronnie added: 'They got Martin back to the morgue and into his coffin before the staff arrived, but the undertaker and his assistants could not understand why there were a load of beer cans on the morgue floor.'

7 Noel Gallagher It was a toss-up which of the Gallagher brothers to include. Both Noel and Liam have drunk a Manchester Ship Canal of booze while turning Oasis into the leaders of the Brit Pop movement. We settled on the older brother because of a series of withering insults dished out towards rivals over the years:

On Blur: 'I hope Damon Albarn and Alex James catch AIDS and die.' (He subsequently made a written apology for this over-the-top statement.)

Keane: 'I'm true to myself – f*** everybody else. What would you rather read? "The guy from Keane's been to a rabbit sanctuary 'cos one of the rabbits needed a kidney transplant, so he swapped his with it" – or "Liam Gallagher sets fire to a policeman in cocaine madness while his brother Noel runs down Oxford Street nude"?'

Robbie Williams: 'The fat dancer from Take That.'

Phil Collins: 'He sells lots of records but makes sh*t albums . . . Vote Labour in the General Election. If the Tories get in Phil Collins is threatening to come back from Switzerland and live in England – none of us want that.'

Collins got his revenge by putting both of the Gallagher brothers into television's *Room 101*. 'They're rude and not as talented as they think they are,' he said with obvious bitterness.

But Noel was never going to let him have the last word: 'Phil Collins knows he can't say anything about me because I'm the f****** dog's bollocks and that's the thing that does his head in . . . and the fact that he's bald.'

George Michael (after the release of his politically slanted single 'Shoot the Dog'): 'He's trying to make social comment. This is the guy who hid who he actually was from the public for twenty years, and now, all of a sudden, he's got something to say about the way of the world. I find it laughable. That's even before you get to his song, which is diabolical.'

Kylie Minogue: 'I don't hate Kylie, but I hate her music with a passion – it's just unbridled filth, it's disgusting.'

Elton John: 'There are precious celebrities who shield themselves from normal public life, saying, "Life is a great thing." Why shut yourself away from it? I can't understand people like Elton John.'

Elton came back with both guns blazing: 'After what f****** Noel Gallagher said about me I couldn't give a sh*t about Oasis. He's just such a tosser, and he looks like Parker from *Thunderbirds*.'

One thing's for sure, the rock scene is more interesting and volatile with the Gallagher brothers around.

6 John Bonham Led Zeppelin could really put the hooch away, with their drummer leading the way. He was once pissed at a Copenhagen art gallery and found himself locked in a discussion about the merits of a particular painting with an overbearing, opinionated critic.

'Want to know what I think of this painting?' Bonham asked, suddenly managing to get a word in.

'Yes, why of course,' said the pain-in-the-arse critic.

Bonham plucked the canvas from the wall and smashed it over the critic's head, then asked: 'Any other painting you'd like me to critique?'

He frequently drank to excess. On 24 September 1980 he started the day with four quadruple vodkas ('My breakfast,' he called it), then continued to drink heavily throughout a rehearsal session. He was carried up to bed in guitarist Jimmy Page's house, and was found dead the following morning. Like fellow-drummer Keith Moon two years earlier, he had died at the age of thirty-two.

But he has left behind a legacy of a beat-heavy style that has influenced a whole generation of drummers.

5 Eric Burdon 'I didn't think I'd see thirty,' admits the Animals' vocalist, having done everything to excess since first forming the band in the early 1960s.

Burdon is almost certainly the inspiration for the 'Eggman' from the Beatles song 'I Am the Walrus'. In his earlier, wild life he was known as 'Eggs' to his friends, because of his fondness for breaking eggs over naked girls. He admitted in his biography that he once did this in the presence of John Lennon, who shouted: 'Go on, go get it, Eggman . . .'

4 Shane MacGowan Hardly a walking advertisement for dentistry, Shane MacGowan would be number one on this list if the criterion was purely a capacity for drink. The Pogues' singer and songwriter is proud to be the king of boozers.

'The most important thing to remember about drunks is that they are far more intelligent than non-drunks,' says one of Ireland's favourite sons. (He was 'accidentally' born in Tunbridge Wells, by the way, but considers himself 100-proof Irish.) 'Drunks spend a lot of time talking in pubs, unlike workaholics who concentrate on their careers and ambitions, who never develop their higher spiritual values, who never explore the insides of their head like a drunk does.'

Time and again people have said that Shane will not make old bones, but he begs to disagree. 'The British press have been giving me six months to live for the past twenty years,' he says. 'But I keep hanging around like a bad smell. They must be getting pissed off interviewing me by now.'

His writing has often been compared to the literary genius Brendan Behan, who also (and this is an understatement) drank to excess. 'I'm just following the Irish tradition of songwriting, the Irish way of life, the human way of life,' he says. 'Cram as much pleasure into life, and rail against the pain you have to suffer as a result. Or scream and rant with the pain, and wait for it to be taken away with beautiful pleasure.'

A little trivia that sits comfortably in this book . . . The Pogues were originally known as Pogue Mahone, but they were persuaded to change their name when appearing on national television. The pressure came from BBC producers who discovered that *pogue mahone* was Irish slang for 'kiss my arse'.

3 Joe Cocker When I was playing the Liverpool pub circuit with the Hi-Fi Three, there was a young singer starting out in the pubs of Sheffield. His stage name was Vance Arnold Cocker and he had formed a band called Vance Arnold and the Avengers. I was a plasterer, Joe a gas-fitter. He went on to become perpetually plastered, and reckons life has always been a gas.

In 1963 he got rave notices when his band supported the Rolling Stones at Sheffield City Hall. That's how long Joe Cocker has been around the rock scene, and he's still going strong, despite trying to drink Britain and the United States dry. He was a major player at the historic Woodstock Festival when he sang 'Delta Lady', 'Some Thing's Goin' On', 'Let's Go Get Stoned', 'I Shall Be Released' and of course his smash-hit version of the Beatles' 'With a Little Help from My Friends'.

Known as the 'Sheffield Soul Shouter', he is a total original in the way he performs, flailing his arms around as if in the middle of a fit. People hearing him without seeing him are often convinced he is black and from the Deep South.

When he appeared on the *Ed Sullivan Show* in 1969, the director tried to hide him behind dancing girls because of his odd body movements. (Shades of when Elvis appeared on the same show and was shown from the waist up so that Middle America would not be offended by his swivelling hips.)

Joe's drinking and drug taking at one time threatened to engulf him, but he came through his self-inflicted crisis and is now a revered elder statesman of the rock world.

2 Ozzy Osbourne Maybe you are surprised that Ozzy – former lead vocalist of the pioneering heavy-metal band Black Sabbath and a hugely successful solo artist – is not number one here. But I reckon even the Prince of Darkness has to bow the knee to Moon the Loon. Nevertheless, Ozzy gave him a run for his money . . .

To celebrate signing his first solo record contract, Ozzy planned to release a flock of white doves at his record company's head office. Allegedly, though, the executives were so indifferent towards Ozzy that he grabbed one of the birds and bit off its head. With blood still dripping from his lips, he was hauled out of the office by a security guard while attempting to decapitate a second dove.

At one point, he was so out of control with his drinking that his wife and manager, Sharon, took all the clothes from his hotel room to prevent him going out on a binge. It took more than that to beat Ozzy. He found one of Sharon's dresses, put it on, went to the nearest pub and got blotto.

While on tour in Texas he was arrested after urinating against the wall of the Alamo. He was drunk . . . and it was eleven o'clock in the morning.

Once he started mixing drugs with his drinks he became virtually insane. He admits that at the depths of his drug addiction, he shot all of the family's seventeen cats. 'Sharon found me under the piano in a white suit, a shotgun in one hand and a knife in the other,' he recalls.

He has cleaned up his act since 1989, when he was arrested for assaulting Sharon while in a drink and drugs haze. But you could still hardly call him 'serene'.

He was in hospital recovering from a near-fatal quadbike crash when his duet of 'Changes' with daughter Kelly went to number one. This set a new record for the longest period between an artist's first UK chart entry and their first number one. His recording of 'Paranoid' with Black Sabbath had peaked at number four in August 1970, thirty-three years earlier.

And in 2005, when inducted into the UK Music Hall of Fame, he was unhappy with the reception he received as he sang with Black Sabbath, so he showed his disgust by mooning the crowd.

Nevertheless, Ozzy's wild-man image was somewhat softened by the reality-TV show *The Osbournes*. He may have set new records for using the f-word, but overall he came across as something of a pussycat and wormed his way into the hearts of millions of American viewers.

Astonishingly for a singer whose albums used to be burned throughout Middle America, the show's success led to him being invited to a White House dinner hosted by President George Bush. When the President mentioned Ozzy by name, the ageing rock legend climbed up on a chair and threw his arms in the air, drawing wild cheers from the VIP audience.

Then, to the man who recorded 'Sabbath Bloody Sabbath', 'Face in Hell' and 'Bloodbath in Paradise', Bush declared, 'Ozzy, Mom loves your stuff.'

It must be the greatest career shift in history: from dove decapitator to favourite of Barbara Bush!

1 Keith Moon We have already taken an in-depth look at the madness of Keith Moon, but he certainly deserves his place at the top of this list, too.

An indication of how far out of it he became was when he broke down in a state of paranoia on hearing a radio DJ introducing the Who's latest hit, 'Substitute'. Keith thought he had been sacked. He could not recognise his own drumming, and was convinced the band had brought in someone else to take his place.

He provided great entertainment in his short life, but sadly there was a very dark side to this Moon.

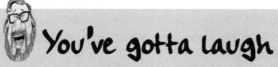# You've gotta laugh

A guy with blond hair walks into a penthouse bar forty storeys up in a Los Angeles skyscraper. As he sits nursing his drink and admiring the panoramic view across the city, he gets talking to a man with jet-black hair who is on the stool alongside him.

'Some view, don't you think?' he asks.

'Yes,' the other man slurs, obviously well on the way to being very drunk. 'But it looks much better on the outside.'

'What do you mean, "on the outside"?'

'You see the alley between this skyscraper and the neighbouring one,' the dark-haired man says, putting on a pair of thick glasses as he looks out of the window.

'Of course I can see it,' says the blond man. 'What's so special about it?'

'Well,' says the dark-haired man, 'there's such a draught coming up between the two buildings that you can jump out of the window and float there.'

The other man nearly spills his drink. 'You've got to be joking,' he says with a laugh.

'I'll prove it to you,' the dark-haired man says, walking boldly, although rather unsteadily, to the window.

The bartender is watching all this, shaking his head as if he has seen and heard it all before.

The dark-haired man removes his spectacles and places them in an inside pocket, pulls open the window and jumps out.

'Oh my God!' the blond man shouts. 'He's gone and committed suic—'

But before he can finish the sentence, the dark-haired man comes floating back up, just as he said he would. He grabs hold of the window frame and pulls himself back into the bar.

'That is the most fantastic thing I've ever seen,' the blond man says. 'I must have a go at this.'

He hands his glass to the barman and then takes a running jump out of the window. There is no sign of him coming back up and the dark-haired man leans out to watch him hitting the pavement below with a splat.

He then walks casually back to the bar and orders another drink.

As the barman places the glass in front of him, he says: 'You can be a real asshole when you're drunk, Superman.'

Hark Who's Talking About Drink

'If drinking is interfering with your work, you're probably a heavy drinker. If work is interfering with your drinking, you're probably an alcoholic.'
– George Bernard Shaw

'Why don't you slip out of those wet clothes and into a dry Martini?'
– Robert Benchley

'He has had so many hangovers that he's now addicted to the hair of the dog.'
– John Edwards

'It takes 7,860 nuts and bolts to assemble a motorcar, and just one drunken nut to scatter it all over the road.'
– Cyril Fletcher

'Drinking releases the inhibitions then, hopefully, the bra strap.'
– Richard Harris

'I was told long ago that you never find the answer to your problems at the bottom of a glass. So now I always drink straight from the bottle.'
– Ronnie Scott

'You know you've had much too much to drink when the ugly barmaid has suddenly got two faces and both of them are beautiful.'
– Dave Allen

'I was once hired to play a drunken customer in a pub, and Olivier said, "Been typecast I see, old chap."'
– Robert Newton

'Wine is fine, beer gives me cheer, sherry causes me to be merry, but it's the whisky that makes me really frisky.'
– Sid Field

'I'm not sure if this is the morning after the night before or the morning after that, but it will all come back to me once I have remembered who I am.'
– Freddie Frinton

'I can't understand people who don't drink. They speak a different language to me.'
– Charlie Drake

'I take twice as long drinking half as much as I used to, and yet I get drunk in half the time. So I am going to try to get drunk more slowly by drinking half as much as I do now in twice the time. Now, to work that little lot out all I have to do is subtract the first drink I thought of. Open the cage.'
– Arthur English

A Shtagger of Famoush Drunksh

My concern throughout this book has been that drinking to excess should not be glorified. A good drink never does anybody any harm, but as the boozers' bible would say: 'Drink enough, never too much.'

As you will see from this chapter, many of the great and the good have succumbed to the temptations of the demon drink and overindulged. Some of their stories will, I hope, give inspiration and motivation to anybody looking for a way to beat the bottle. Others will act as a warning that it might be wise to say 'no' to that next drink.

Unless you drink sensibly, alcohol can suddenly jump up and bite you on the arse!

Ben Affleck An actor who has crowded a lot into his young life (he was born on 15 August 1972), Ben has starred in *Good Will Hunting*, *Armaggedon*, *Shakespeare in Love* and *Pearl Harbor*, romanced renowned beauties such as Jennifer Lopez, Gwyneth Paltrow and Jennifer Garner (whom he married), and has recently proved himself one of the best poker players on the West Coast.

Sadly, along the way, he also picked up a drinking habit. It was his good friend and fellow-imbiber Charlie Sheen who drove him to a rehab centre for urgent treatment. Ben's father also fought an addiction battle, and he is now a counsellor who has helped his son as well as many other recovering alcoholics.

Ben is noted among his peers as one of the finest impersonators in Hollywood. While filming *The Sum of All Fears* in 2002 he made a close study of his co-star Morgan Freeman and got his voice off so perfectly that Morgan said: 'Man, you ever do that again, I'll kill you! Even I thought you were me.'

In future, the multi-talented Ben knows he must only impersonate drunks and not be one for real. As he once said, 'A full life awaits me without alcohol.'

Buzz Aldrin The second man on the moon has famously been a recovering alcoholic for more than twenty years, and has poured himself into a campaign aimed at helping others beat the bottle. He believes it is important for prominent celebrities

Buzz Aldrin was often spaced out because of his out-of-control boozing.

like himself to 'appear in public and be proud of their status of recovery'.

He says: 'It's like a bank account: you're accumulating sobriety and you're accumulating a desire to protect that. There's a risk if someone wants to be known as recovering and then have their ego boosted that they can then trip and fall. But I am happy to speak of my own experiences if it will help anybody out there with the disease – and that is what it is – of alcoholism.'

Buzz traces the origins of his problem back to his mother and father: 'I had two parents who had traits of alcoholism in varying degrees and it adversely affected my mother's life in particular.'

His sudden celebrity status brought pressures that Buzz relieved through drink. 'You gain a degree of notoriety,' he says, 'and you begin not to be able to do things without people knowing what you're doing; you're more on show.'

On his return from the historic 1969 moon landing with Neil Armstrong, Buzz found himself fêted around the world. He was forced on a celebratory tour and held up as an example of excellence and high achievement. A military man through and through, the tour gave him a degree of freedom that was a shock after so many years of strict, regimented discipline. Buzz says: 'The way I dealt with it was to use alcohol, as everyone does, to socially loosen up, to be lubricated. But the thing is a bit more pronounced with those of us who are alcoholics. I felt imposed on by a sudden new set of conditions and I guess maybe that led to a sense of frustration and depression.'

It took Buzz a few years to realise that he was battling not only depression but alcoholism, and that the two problems formed a vicious circle.

He stresses the importance of recovery programmes for alcoholics: 'I think recovery organisations are essential. I still participate in that because I enjoy the sharing that takes place and the friendship.'

And he appreciates that society's understanding of alcoholism as a disease has come a long way in the last fifty years. 'It used to be an unacceptable thing,' he says. 'People were just too proud to ever acknowledge that something they were doing was inappropriate or maybe adversely affecting their lives.'

For Buzz, his achievement in remaining sober is perhaps even greater than the one that made him famous in 1969.

Tim Allen There is a tragic irony in the *Home Improvement* star going into rehab for a drink-dependency problem in 1997 because it was the consequence of an arrest for drink-driving. The chilling fact is that when he was just eleven years old his father was knocked down and killed by a drunk driver.

Tallulah Bankhead This actress from a powerful American political family was notorious as 'one of the wildest women of the twentieth century', and between film-making and stage appearances she managed to squeeze in dozens of scandals because of her drunken behaviour and seemingly insatiable sexual appetite. She once felt the gaze of a lord of the realm on her while at a Washington cocktail party. 'What's the matter, dahling?' she purred for all the room to hear. 'Don't you recognise me with my clothes on?'

She boasted late in life that she had slept with more than five thousand people (of both sexes), including Marlene Dietrich. Her favourite party piece was to strip naked in a crowded room and dance in Asian style before miming positions from the *Kama Sutra*.

She almost died in 1933 after contracting gonorrhoea. 'It was either from George Raft or Gary Cooper,' she casually claimed, citing two of the biggest Hollywood stars of the time.

It emerged in recently declassified papers that MI5 had investigated her. The allegation was that she had corrupted pupils at Eton after seducing half a dozen of them in a romp in her suite at a Berkshire hotel during a visit to England when she was thirty-two. The investigators failed to prove anything because 'of the obstructive attitude of the Headmaster whose only interest was in protecting Eton from scandal'.

The last word on her lips when she died in 1968 aged sixty-five was 'bourbon'.

Brendan Behan Poet, novelist, short-story writer, playwright (a brilliant stylist in both Gaelic and English), Brendan Behan was a master at everything he turned his hand to . . . including the art of drinking. This committed Irish Republican described himself as 'a drinker with a writing problem', and claimed, 'I only drink on two occasions – when I'm thirsty and when I'm not.'

One of the most gifted writers of his generation, he was hired by Guinness to come up with a slogan. A dozen kegs of the black stuff were sent over as part payment in advance. After six weeks and no slogan, a company representative contacted him and asked what he had come up with. Thinking quickly on unsteady feet, Brendan – who, of course, had already consumed all of his advance – said: 'Guinness makes you drunk.' (It has since been claimed that he coined the more memorable 'Guinness is good for you', but in fact that was the work of Dorothy L. Sayers.)

To those who criticised his excessive drinking, he retorted: 'Where I come from, to get enough to eat is an achievement. To get enough to get drunk is a victory.'

He was a soldier in the IRA and it was reported that he had been court-martialled for going absent without leave. 'Yes, that is true,' he confirmed. 'I was court-martialled in my absence, and sentenced to death in my absence. So I said, "Go ahead and shoot me . . . in my absence!"'

Desperate for a drink, he once entered a priest's house and begged for something alcoholic – 'Communal wine will suffice, if that's all you have, Father.'

The priest provided him with a little Irish whiskey in a glass, saying he felt guilty because 'I am tapping a nail into your coffin.'

Brendan reportedly looked at the meagre amount and said: 'You wouldn't mind giving the nail another tap would you, Father?'

This great writer and wit took too many liberties with alcohol and died in Dublin aged just forty-one. But he retained his sense of humour right to the end. His famous last words – to a nun – were: 'May all your sons be bishops.'

Jeffrey Bernard This celebrated drunk was immortalised in the play *Jeffrey Bernard Is Unwell* by Keith Waterhouse. He used to get so hopelessly paralytic living what he described as 'the low life in Soho' that when he failed to submit his column for the *Spectator* the editor would insert the line, 'Jeffrey Bernard is unwell.' Regular readers knew precisely which illness was meant.

When he did manage to produce something the results were frequently hilarious, albeit forming 'a suicide note in weekly instalments'. Rival magazine *Private Eye* added to the Bernard legend with a cartoon series in which pub regulars would invariably ask: 'Jeffbinin?'

Married four times, he described alcohol as 'the other woman'.

George Best We have already devoted plenty of pages to him, but there is always room for one more George Best story.

It seems remarkable, considering the on-the-edge lifestyle he led, that George went to prison only once. This was his rock bottom in 1984 when, having failed to appear in court on a drink-driving charge and resisting arrest after the police had trapped him in a girlfriend's flat, he served two months.

Only George could have found humour in the situation when moments after being sentenced at Southwark Crown Court he said to his solicitor: 'Well, I suppose that's the knighthood fucked!'

Humphrey Bogart As we saw earlier, Bogie was the founder of the Rat Pack, and he set great drinking standards for his successors: Frank Sinatra, Dean Martin, Sammy Davis Jnr and the rest. But his screen image of a streetwise tough guy was in direct contrast to the real Bogart. He was born into an American upper-crust family, and after private schooling he trained at medical school before being hooked first by Broadway and then by Hollywood.

One of the many rumours about him was that he got his trade-mark scar and lisp when a prisoner he was guarding during naval service in the First World War smashed him in the face with his handcuffs. A more salacious version was that he had been gashed during a drunken scuffle with a jealous husband who had stabbed him with a broken beer bottle.

His drinking pal David Niven revealed the more innocent truth on a television chat show: 'Bogie's lisp and scar were caused when a splinter of wood became embedded in his lower lip when he was a kid. He told me [and here, Niven performed a perfect impersonation of Bogie]: "Goddam doctor – instead of stitching it up, he screwed it up."'

Richard Burton A master actor and king of drinkers, Richard Burton's CV is conspicuously blank for the year 1959. That's because he took twelve months off as a result of what happened on a drunken night out in a London pub with fellow-Welshman and fellow-imbiber Dylan Thomas several years before.

After a poetry-reading session for BBC Radio in 1952, Burton and Thomas joined friends in a pub near the studio. A drunken Irishman in the

Richard Burton, whose drink problems were possibly Taylor-made.

bar said he specialised in reading palms, and the two Welshmen joined in the fun. The drunk predicted the year of death for Thomas, Burton and three of their friends. Thomas was told 1953, and he duly died while on a tour of the United States on 9 November 1953. Over the next few years the three other friends also all died in the year predicted by the drunk. Unsurprisingly, Burton began to worry about *his* year, 1959.

So he decided to take the year off rather than tempt fate, and proved he meant it when he turned down $350,000 to star as Jesus in Nicholas Ray's remake of *King of Kings*.

Burton survived the year and lived until 5 August 1984, although he fought a recurring battle with alcoholism for the rest of his life.

George W. Bush Who do you believe? The President, who says he has not had a drink since quitting in 1986? Or his political enemies who claim there is plenty of evidence to suggest he still hits the bottle?

An arrest for drink-driving in 1976 was covered up until just one week before his first bid for the presidency in 2000. It was dismissed as dirty tricks by his opponents and he squeezed into the White House after winning the dodgy deciding vote in Florida, where his brother just happens to be the Governor.

Stories have since been leaked about him binge drinking when at college, and there was an extraordinary claim that he had once drunkenly challenged his father (the first President Bush) to a '*mano-a-mano*' fight while being bollocked for another drink-driving incident.

Recently, a 1992 video surfaced that showed Bush looking much the worse for wear and slurring his speech during a private wedding reception, and family members have said he also turned to drink during the Hurricane Katrina crisis of 2005.

But the President insists he has been dry since waking up with a bad hangover following his fortieth birthday party celebrations. He says he has been influenced by the teachings of the Reverend Billy Graham and a renewed belief in the Bible.

It is purely a personal opinion, but many of his decisions since he got into the White House seem to suggest he is still on the sauce.

Lord Byron Lady Caroline Lamb famously described him as 'mad, bad and dangerous to know', and the noble lord could hardly argue. When he was barely twenty and studying at Cambridge University, he used to order bottles of port, claret and sherry by the dozen. As he later wrote: 'Man, being reasonable, must get drunk; the best of life is but intoxication.' I couldn't have put it better myself!

His heroes rarely had a glass too far out of reach. His approach to life was captured by the words he put into the mouth of Don Juan: 'Let us have wine and women, mirth and laughter; Sermons and soda-water the day after.'

When a Scottish critic savaged one of his poems, Byron got as drunk as a lord by sinking three bottles of claret and dashing out the satire *English Bards and Scotch Reviewers*.

His regular drinking partner was the playwright and politician Richard Sheridan, but Byron also found the time to hop in and out of many ladies' boudoirs. He was also known to be fond of young boys.

Following his exile in Italy, he was so desperate not to become obese that he lived on a diet of red cabbage washed down with hock or cider. He was just thirty-six when he died in 1824 while trying to stir up a revolution in Greece.

Truman Capote One of the finest American writers of modern times, the author of *Breakfast at Tiffany's* and *In Cold Blood* was rarely cold sober at the peak of his career.

He stood just five foot four, was balding, had a high-pitched voice and lisp, and was openly gay when it was not only unfashionable but positively dangerous to be so. He claimed to have had flings with dozens of celebrities, including Errol Flynn.

I would love to have been a witness when he was on the set of *Beat the Devil* in 1953, squaring up to Humphrey Bogart. Bogie was the star of the film, Capote the screenwriter. This is how Truman recalled it during an interview in 1974:

Bogart was a very good friend of mine. He was one of those people who loved to come around and give you big hugs and punches and things like that all in the name of joviality. On this particular morning I was suffering a terrible hangover after a drinking session with the director John Huston and Bogie. It had obviously not upset Bogie like it had me and he sort of came up and gave me this big clap on the back, and I told him to stop that. 'Don't do that again,' I said, meaning it. And he said, 'What's the matter with you, anyway?' And he did it again. So I said, 'OK, don't say I didn't warn you.' I just

*took my foot and put it behind his leg and gave him a good
push. He fell down and broke his arm. This caused the film
to go about $200,000 over budget because he couldn't work
for several weeks. I was not the most popular man in the film
studio.*

What you might call Capote kaput!

Johnny Cash 'The Man in Black' was in a mess in the 1960s through
a dangerous mix of alcohol and amphetamines, and it came to a head
at the Grand Ole Opry in Nashville. He lost control during a concert and
dragged the mike stand across the front of the stage, smashing every
one of the fifty-two floor lights. Johnny was asked to leave the stage,
and was on the venue's banned list for several years until he got himself straightened out.

After failing with a suicide attempt in 1967, he was pulled
back from the edge by his singing partner June Carter and they married a year later. He later found God and became a dedicated
Christian.

He recalled that the weirdest thing that happened to him during his
alcohol- and drug-fuelled days was when he accidentally set fire to a
forest. His truck broke down with a defective exhaust and flying sparks
set off the blaze. Within moments everything around him was aflame,
and the fire eventually destroyed 508 acres and burned all the foliage
off the trees on three mountains.

'I was arrested,' said Cash, 'and in court the judge asked, "Why did
you do it?"

'I said, "It wasn't me, it was my truck. And as it's dead, you can't
question it." It finished up with me being sued for $125,000 which I got
down to $82,000 on appeal. The state I was in back in those days, it
was enough to drive me to drink.'

I wonder if that's where he got the inspiration for 'Ring of Fire'?

Raymond Chandler Thriller writer Raymond Chandler created the immortal, hard-living, hard-drinking private eye Philip Marlowe. That was fiction. In the real world, Chandler lived harder and drank even more than his imagined hero.

Born in the USA but raised in London, Chandler was on the slope towards being an alcoholic from his days fighting with the Canadian Army in the First World War. (He had crossed back to the other side of the Atlantic because he detested the British Civil Service job into which he had been pushed by his family.) He later revealed that during the war he drank so much that he regularly blacked out.

By 1932, he had risen to a vice-president's job with an oil syndicate in California, but he was fired because of his drinking in the aftermath of a suicide attempt that he'd made during one of his many manic depressions.

But he had a burning ambition to become a writer, and was encouraged by the publication in 1933 of his short story *Blackmailers Don't Shoot*. His big breakthrough came with the publication of the novel *The Big Sleep* in 1939. He was suddenly in demand as a Hollywood screenwriter and produced scripts for *Double Indemnity*, *The Blue Dahlia* and Hitchcock's *Strangers on a Train*. He and Hitchcock disliked each other, and Chandler used to call out, 'Where's the fat bastard?' when walking on set, knowing full well that the great director could hear him.

He had a complicated love life, with lots of women in the mix and – according to some – a man or two as well.

After writing the classic *The Long Goodbye* he lost himself in the bottle, dying in a Californian hospital in March 1959. He proposed marriage to his literary agent Helga Green on his deathbed, keeping his life dramatic to the very last chapter.

As Philip Marlowe once said: 'Dead men weigh more than broken hearts.' The women in his life said of the author who penned those words, 'Farewell my lovely.'

Winston Churchill I have already discussed how Winston's family protect his image by saying his drinking has been greatly exaggerated. But too many of his contemporaries witnessed his enormous intake for there to be any doubt that he was a Premiership-class boozer.

He was nicely warmed by brandy when in Fulton, Missouri, in March 1946 for the dedication of a bust in his honour. Revealing the sculpture to polite applause, he said to an aide: 'What Hitler would have given to have seen my head on a plinth like that.'

A woman then came forward from the crowd and shook him warmly by the hand. 'Mr Churchill,' she said, 'this is such an honour. I have travelled a hundred miles this morning for the unveiling of your bust.'

'Madam, I assure you,' lisped Winston, 'in that regard I would gladly return the favour!'

Eric Clapton Britain's greatest living rock guitarist (or just plain 'God' to his fans) admits that there was a time in his career when he could not perform on stage unless he was drunk. 'In my blithering idiot days,' he confesses, 'I was drinking three bottles of vodka a day and being carried around. I also kept stashes of booze hidden in my car. It was crazy.'

Having already beaten a heroin addiction, Eric set about coming to terms with his alcoholism in a life that has been one hell of a rollercoaster trip. 'My life has been chaotic,' he admits, 'like something out of a Fellini film.'

That was understandable when you consider how it started. He was brought up with a girl he thought was his older sister, but later it was revealed that she was in fact his mother. He never knew his father, a Canadian soldier.

What I admire about Eric is that he goes out of his way to help those who have travelled similar roads to his own. For instance, in 1998 he opened the Crossroads Centre, a rehabilitation facility to provide care for some of the poorest people in the Caribbean with drink and drug dependency problems. He raised five million dollars for the centre by auctioning off a hundred guitars, and he regularly hosts concerts to keep funds topped up.

Nicknamed 'Slowhand', in his youth he was anything but slow at tilting back glasses, and he has also dated some of the world's most beautiful women, including Sharon Stone, Naomi Campbell and Sheryl Crow.

Now sober in his seventh decade, he says he no longer turns women's heads. 'I don't flirt with them the way I used to,' he recently revealed, 'because I don't want them to think I'm a dirty old man. In many ways it's a relief not to be ruled by my sex drive.'

Montgomery Clift Already hooked on booze and drugs, Montgomery Clift's life and career went into free-fall after he survived a car crash while filming *Raintree County* with Elizabeth Taylor in 1956. Taylor was his closest friend, and she may well have saved his life in the immediate aftermath of the crash. One of the first on the scene, she pulled two teeth out of his throat, where they had been restricting his breathing.

Although lucky to be alive, the handsome actor never came to terms with being disfigured as a result of his injuries, and his descent into alcoholism was described as 'his long suicide'. He eventually died ten years later at the age of forty-five, hopelessly lost in the bottle.

He received an Oscar nomination for his 1961 performance in *Judgment at Nuremberg*, but he remembered little of his seven-minute appearance in the film. Stanley Kramer, the director, gave a remarkable insight into Clift's performance:

Montgomery arrived on the film set looking like a haunted, broken man. He struggled to remember his lines even for the one short scene in which he appeared as a witness, and we had to go for retake after retake. Finally I said to him, 'Just forget the damn lines,

Monty. Let's say you're on the witness stand. The prosecutor says something to you, then the defence attorney bitterly attacks you, and you have to reach for a word in the script. Just go for it. Any key word that comes to mind. Whatever the word may be, it doesn't really matter. Just turn to Spencer [Tracy] on the bench whenever you feel the need, and ad-lib something. It will be all right because it will convey the confusion in your character's mind.' Monty seemed to calm down after this. He wasn't always close to the script, but whatever he said fitted in perfectly, and he came through with a performance good enough to convince the Academy that he deserved an Oscar nomination. But I'll tell you this, Monty was so far gone that he could not have told you one thing that he said on that set. It was so sad to see.

A year later Clift was sued by studio bosses for his continual absences from the set when shooting *Freud* with John Huston.

He and Marlon Brando were both born in Omaha, Nebraska, and they became lifelong screen rivals. Many considered Clift at least Brando's equal as an actor until the crash that virtually destroyed not only his looks but his soul.

Peter Cook In a 2005 poll conducted on both sides of the Atlantic, Peter Cook was voted the funniest comedian of all time, ahead of the likes of Woody Allen, Groucho Marx, Laurel and Hardy, Eric Morecambe and Bob Hope. He would also have come close to winning the 'comedian who sank the most booze' award.

He hit the self-destruct button after his one-time comedy partner Dudley Moore secured fame and fortune in Hollywood, and his slow descent into alcoholism was horrific to watch for those who knew of his secret vice.

The viciously funny *Derek and Clive* recordings were made when Cook was overloaded, and he showed his cruel side by trying to belittle a virtually defenceless Moore in almost every sentence. He had the uncanny ability to act sober the minute the red light came on in the studio, having arrived less than an hour earlier hardly able to stand.

Peter was a true comic genius. He wrote the hilarious 'One Legged Tarzan' sketch when still a teenager, and as owner and founder of *Private Eye* he had a profound influence on satirical humour for four decades, writing for the magazine under his pen name Lord Gnome.

But he had no time for the 'celebrity circus', as he called it. A reportedly true story that summarises his dislike of that world is provided by Sir David Frost, one of the co-founders of the British satire scene in the early sixties.

Frost phoned Cook and said, 'Peter, I'm having a little dinner party on behalf of Prince Andrew and his new bride-to-be Sarah Ferguson. I know they'd love to meet you. They are big fans. Be super if you could make it: Wednesday the twelfth.'

'Hang on . . . I'll just check my diary,' Cook replied agreeably. There was a pause and the sound of pages being turned. 'Oh dear,' he finally said in exaggerated apologetic tones. 'I'm afraid I'm watching television that night.'

Joan Crawford One of the great icons of the film industry, Joan Crawford went all the way from elevator operator to the top of the Hollywood heap. It was a well-lubricated ride, but her drinking became a huge problem only on the downward spiral, when she was sinking a quart bottle of vodka a day.

Joan was christened Lucille Fay Le Sueur, but MGM boss Louis B. Mayer insisted on the change, 'otherwise people will be calling her "the sewer"'. She was given her new name in a readers' competition run by a movie magazine.

Throughout her long career she had an intense rivalry with Bette Davis, and when they appeared together in *Whatever Happened to Baby Jane?* the off-camera atmosphere was said to be Arctic.

Davis once said of Joan, who was renowned for 'putting it about a bit': 'She's slept with every male star at MGM except Lassie.'

Crawford's reply was more subtle, but no less barbed: 'I don't hate Bette Davis, even though the press wants me to. I resent her. I don't see how she built a career out of a set of mannerisms, instead of real acting ability. Take away the pop eyes, the cigarette, and those funny clipped words and what have you got? She's phoney, but I guess the public really likes that.' Miaoooow!

As well as an addiction to alcohol, Joan had what would now be called obsessive-compulsive disorder. She used to wash her hands every ten minutes and follow guests around her house wiping everything they touched, especially doorknobs and pieces of china. When she found a workman had used her toilet, she had it ripped out and a new one put in its place!

One of her four adopted children, Christina, put the blade in after Joan died in 1977 at the age of seventy-seven. She wrote a kick-and-tell book (later turned into a film) called *Mommie Dearest*, in which she exposed emotional and physical abuse by a mother painted as a raging egomaniac.

How sad that Miss Le Sueur's fame brought her such misery. I prefer to remember her as a sultry actress who used to light up the silver screen as a minx in mink.

John Daly It takes some doing to transcend the genteel world of golf and become known as 'The Wild Thing'. John Daly has achieved this in a headline-hitting career that has been continually interrupted by alcohol-related controversy.

He was once removed from a British Airways plane by airport security for harassing a flight attendant while drunk, and he has even appeared boozed on the course during tournaments. During one in Vancouver in 1998 he was visibly shaking as he tried to play.

Daly once claimed that he drank a fifth of Jack Daniel's every day in his early twenties, and he has continued to fight his demons ever since. He caused uproar among the golf community in 1994 when he stated that many PGA golfers are cocaine users, adding that if drug testing were done on tour he would be 'one of the cleanest guys out there'.

Recently, he has started to get his act together after confessing that he had frittered away more than $50 million gambling, including an extraordinary single day in Las Vegas when he managed to go through $1.5 million, most of it lost on the $5,000-a-go slot machines.

One of the most exciting golfers ever – particularly off the tee – Daly can hit the ball prodigious distances, putting his huge bulk into his drives. The one thing he has not conquered is an ever-increasing waistline. The former British Open champion declined the annual invitation to the past-champions' banquet (a black-tie event) because 'you don't get a guy this big into a suit'.

Appropriately, a 'John Daly' cocktail has been created. It's an Arnold Palmer (lemonade and iced tea) mixed with a large whisky and a splash of ginger ale.

Edward VIII As much as the Establishment try to hush it up, it is an open secret that the woman for whom Edward VIII gave up his throne eventually drove him to drink. There must have been something about that Wallis Simpson, because her first husband also became a helpless alcoholic.

In official papers released sixty-five years after the Abdication, it was revealed that she had a steamy affair with future German Foreign Minister, Joachim von Ribbentrop. This was when he was Ambassador to London in 1936 – the very year that Edward became King and quit before his coronation to be with 'the woman he loved'. Von Ribbentrop used to send her seventeen carnations every day to remind her of the number of times they had slept together. An FBI investigation in 1941 found that she was passing information to her former lover while London was being blitzed.

A few years later the Duchess of Windsor (as she was by then) started a torrid affair with Jimmy Donahue, the playboy grandson of zillionaire F.W. Woolworth. She was fifty-four; he was thirty-four ... and, until then, a promiscuous homosexual.

No wonder the poor old Duke hit the bottle. He once sank so much brandy that doctors had to use a stomach pump on him.

Keith Floyd Our television sets were in danger of failing the breathalyser test when Keith Floyd was cooking (and drinking) in his peak years as a celebrity chef with a huge appetite for sauce of the alcoholic variety.

Keith used to take huge slurps of vino, and lashings of wine seemed to be an essential element in all his recipes. He used to insist that a lot of it was an act, but the impression was that he'd gone down the same booze-lubricated road as Graham Kerr, the 'Galloping Gourmet' who is now a recovering alcoholic.

There was sad evidence that Floyd was still hitting the bottle when, aged sixty, he was found to be well over the limit when pranging his car in Swindon. He got a driving ban and a hefty £1,500 fine, then came out with a strong statement condemning drink-driving. 'My message is very clear and very simple: too many people do not realise that if they have been drinking the night before, one drink the next day can top them up,' he warned. 'My advice is enjoy yourselves, but get pissed at home and don't even think of driving.'

Sharon Gless One half of the hugely popular *Cagney and Lacey* double act, actress Sharon Gless had the courage and character to tell the world she had become drink dependent.

This was after her agent Ronnie Myre had taken the tough decision to confront her with the blunt truth. Interviewed for the BBC series *Booze*, Sharon said:

Sharon Gless liked a glass or three, and had the courage to own up to it.

Ronnie sounded quite sombre when inviting me out for dinner, and I was convinced he was going to tell me that I was putting on weight. We were sitting in this Malibu restaurant. It was a very 'in' restaurant and there were lots of showbiz people there.

I said, 'I know you're taking me to dinner because you think I'm putting on weight.'

He looked at me and shook his head a little. Then he said: 'No, that isn't why I'm taking you to dinner actually. I invited you to dinner because I love you.'

And I said: 'Well, I love you too.'

Then he said: 'And I think you're an alcoholic.'

*I remember saying: 'Stop it, stop this, everybody is looking at me,'
and I was crying.*

*Ronnie said: 'Let them look, I don't care. I may lose you as a client
and I may lose you as a friend, but I'm afraid I'm going to lose you.'*

I think he thought I was going to die.

It was the wake-up call that Sharon needed. She checked into a rehab
centre and started the fight back.

She had her last drink more than fifteen years ago, and now does not
dwell on her alcoholism, saying: 'I don't think about it very much, to be
honest with you. It means not having to wonder what time it is, is it time
to have a drink? It means not having people judge me or counting how
many glasses are in front of me. It's just a lot simpler this way. I was
lucky to get out when I did.'

And the world is lucky to have a lady brave enough to talk about her
problem. What a role model for all those who may be dipping too much
into the alcoholic well.

God bless yer, Sharon Gless.

Jimmy Greaves He may not have touched a drop since 20 February
1978, his thirty-eighth birthday, but Greavsie is still one of the most
famous drunks in British footballing history, mainly because he did
so much of his drinking when he was at the pinnacle of the game.
I know the exact date when he stopped because Jimmy's writing
partner Norman Giller – who also happens to be my collaborator on
the *My Arse* series – gave up drinking the very same day.

'I wanted to encourage Jimmy to beat the bottle, so I stopped
too,' says 'Saint' Norman. 'In those days football reporters and
players regularly got rat-arsed with each other without the hacks
writing a word about it in their newspapers. Today's "celebrity"
footballers, with their hundred-grand-a-week wages, don't allow
reporters anywhere near them, and most football journalists are
looked on not as friend but foe.'

Greavsie is in this list because he is a shining example of what can be achieved. Throughout most of the seventies he was an undependable, unreliable drunk. But – with the initial help of Alcoholics Anonymous – he won back his life and his family, and he had the character to start a new career as a hugely popular and witty television personality, chatting about the game he played better than almost anybody else on the planet. He remains in the public eye as one of the funniest 'water-only' after-dinner speakers you will ever hear.

Larry Hagman While rolling in make-believe oil as the scheming J.R. Ewing in *Dallas*, actor Larry Hagman was continually getting well oiled. Then came the frightening moment of truth. On a routine medical check-up he was told by his doctor that, as a direct result of his heavy drinking, he had cirrhosis of the liver. He was suddenly faced with the prospect that another alcoholic drink could kill him.

'Right there and then I poured my vodka away and decided that the drinking days were over,' he said.

Larry had enjoyed a long run of drinking his fill, having started years before he became J.R., when he was the genial star of *I Dream of Jeannie*. 'I was loaded all the time,' he admitted. 'I was loaded all the way through *Jeannie* and all during *Dallas*.' At the peak of his drinking (and fame) he was getting through three bottles of champagne every day during filming.

Like George Best, Larry was given a second shot at life with a liver transplant; but, unlike Georgie, he made the most of it. Now he preaches against drinking too much of the hard stuff. He has also quit smoking and is a leading spokesperson for the anti-tobacco lobby in the United States.

Larry was so wacky in his drinking days that he was known in his local neighbourhood as the 'Mad Monk of Malibu', and although he isn't boozing any more, the eccentricity lives on. He has drawn up plans for his funeral to be three days of feasting and fun. And all his friends will eventually receive a special cake. 'When I die,' he says, 'I want my friends to eat me. I want to be fed through a wood chipper, be spread over a wheat field, then have a cake baked from the crop for all my pals to munch on. We will sprinkle in a little marijuana to give it a bit of a kick!'

Jet Harris A pioneering bass player with the Shadows (Cliff Richard's backing band) in the 1950s, Terence 'Jet' Harris lost his way in an alcoholic fog at what should have been the peak of his career. He provided the unique bass line on such huge hits as 'Apache', but confesses that the only thing he was thinking about during sell-out concerts was the next drink: 'The other boys looked forward to a drink for enjoyment,' he recalls. 'For me the drink became a necessity.'

He shocked the rock world in 1962 by quitting the Shadows at the summit of their success. Initially it seemed like a good move when he had a solo hit with 'Diamonds', but then he became the pawn of alcohol and almost lost his life in a car smash that left him with serious head injuries.

As the music work dried up he took a series of menial, making-ends-meet jobs, including bus conductor, potato planter, brickie and hospital porter. When his third marriage ended in 1989, he was on the dole and a seemingly helpless alcoholic.

He just about remembers his rock-bottom moment after a drinking binge in London with Rod Stewart and Jeff Beck. He woke up in a car park, trying to make sense of his surroundings.

'It was winter,' he recalls, 'and all I knew from my watch was that it was six o'clock. But six o'clock in the morning or six o'clock in the evening? I had no idea whatsoever.'

Suddenly, out of the misery he found hope when he met his present wife Janet at a Hank Marvin concert. She gave him the desire and the determination to beat the bottle. As he got his monsters under control, he regained his appetite for playing and now lends his unique bass sound to anyone wise enough to want it.

His story gives hope to all those who think they are losing their battle with the bottle.

Ernest Hemingway Widely considered to be America's most influential writer of the twentieth century, just the name Ernest Hemingway conjures up images of bullfights and bar-room brawls, deep-sea fishing, big-game hunting . . . and booze binges. His is a legend as steeped in alcohol as it is in adventure.

Read almost any of his books and you will find a reflection of the author's life. All of his heroes loved and drank hard, and a glass and a bottle were rarely out of reach, either for them or for the genius who was creating them.

I wonder how many readers Hemingway started on the slippery slope to alcoholism by making boozing to excess seem cool and glamorous? His well-documented days in Paris were alcohol-fuelled, as the outstanding writers and artists of the time flocked to join him in his soirées on the Left Bank – a million miles away from the sober climate of Prohibition America. At any one time the brightest minds of what became known as the Lost Generation could be found in this circle – F. Scott Fitzgerald out of his head on champagne, Ezra Pound and Gertrude Stein guzzling wine, James Joyce getting stuck into the Scotch with 'Papa' Hemingway, the daddy of them all.

It was decades before discerning critics armed with hindsight described their excessive drinking as a plague on the era rather than a catalyst. However, as Fitzgerald noted, 'Sometimes I wish I'd gone through those good times stone cold sober so I could remember everything – but then again, if I had been sober the times probably wouldn't have been worth remembering.'

So as not to contribute to the glorification of Hemingway's immense capacity for alcohol, here's an anecdote that shows how too much booze can turn even the most towering intellectual into a fool.

Hemingway had a scar on his forehead that many people thought he must have collected while fighting bulls or during his First World War service as an ambulanceman. But no, he got it when – pissed out of his head – he pulled what he thought was a toilet chain and managed to drag a skylight down on to his head!

John Hurt In a career spanning more than forty years, John Hurt has consistently proved himself one of the outstanding actors on stage and screen. But this Man for All Seasons was often an off-screen drunk during every season, and he has made a Herculean effort to conquer his demons. His full and eventful life has been a hair-raising adventure during which he has had to hide a darker, self-destructive side, with alcohol as his constant enemy.

By nature he is a gentle, sophisticated man, with a father who was a vicar, a mother who was a teacher, and a brother who became a monk. But on the screen he can do it all: outrageously gay (*The Naked Civil Servant*), menacing and debauched (*I, Claudius*), junkie (*Midnight Express*), high-society pimp (*Scandal*). And who can forget his astonishing performance as the Elephant Man?

His greatest achievement was getting himself dry after years of drinking, but he slipped off the wagon spectacularly in 2004 before and during London's Empire Film Awards. The sixty-four-year-old actor made tabloid headlines when he was ejected from a lap-dancing bar after being accused of drunk and offensive behaviour, and then made a sad spectacle of himself at the awards bash at the Dorchester Hotel. He presented a 'Career Achievement' award to *Alien* co-star Sigourney Weaver, but struggled to read from the autocue as he introduced her. He was all over the place, and made a complete hash of it.

There have been rumours about Hurt's sexuality ever since he made such a convincing job of portraying Quentin Crisp in *The Naked Civil Servant* (in spite of the fact that he has been married *four* times). And he did little to quell the gossip when, clearly the worse for wear, he told two female reporters from the *Daily*

Mirror: 'I like to dress up in women's clothing. Every man wants to be a woman, and ones who deny it are lying. I'd love to be a woman. They have beautiful clothes – all soft blouses and pretty skirts. I like dressing up.'

Slurring his words, he then went on to proposition the journalists, asking: 'Do you girls offer yourselves, do you, do you? You're a naughty one. What are we going to do with you? I bet you've got really big nipples. Show me.'

It Hurts to see a fine actor in such a state.

Billy Joel This exceptional singer, pianist and songwriter came into the new millennium battling drink demons, checking in and out of hospitals and the Betty Ford Clinic as he struggled to get his alcoholism under control. He confessed that when hitting rock bottom he tried to commit suicide by drinking furniture polish after an affair with his drummer's wife left him feeling guilty and manically depressed.

The rock legend has wrecked three cars in crashes that his concerned friends and fans fear have been alcohol-related. One clue was that he gave permission for a radio station to auction the third wreck – with any profits going to raise money for an anti-drink-driving campaign.

But in 2007 Billy proved that he was beating his drink problem, packing theatres and stadiums during a triumphant United States tour. The Piano Man had turned things around, becoming another celebrity who gives hope to anybody fighting the booze battle.

Charles Kennedy Poor old Charlie suffered with his drinking problem in the full glare of the political publicity machine, and in Westminster no mercy is shown to anybody with a weakness . . . not if there are votes to be snatched.

He might have got away with it on the backbenches (plenty of those noisy beggars seem permanently pissed to me!), but as leader of the Lib-Dems he was there – to coin a phrase – to be hung out to dry.

His undoing was almost like watching a public suicide. It came at the manifesto launch on his first day back on the campaign trail after the birth of his son. In the full view of the television cameras, Charlie struggled to remember the details of a key tax policy and seemed confused and distracted throughout.

He later blamed his performance on lack of sleep due to the demands of his new baby, but the Fleet Street Rottweilers were on the case (the case of whisky, perhaps?) and he eventually had to come clean and step down from the leadership.

Charlie remains one of the wittiest and most likeable politicians in the House, and everybody – including his opponents – is rooting for him to win his battle.

Mario Lanza One of the most distinctive voices of the twentieth century, Mario Lanza made a huge impact in his short, thirty-eight-year lifespan. He had a soaring tenor voice which many considered rivalled that of the great Caruso, whom he portrayed on screen in one of his blockbusting films.

But he had a volcanic temper and lost it on set during the filming of 1954's *The Student Prince*. The director told him he was singing 'Beloved' with too much passion. Lanza went berserk, saying that he was willing to have his acting directed but *not* his singing. He stormed off set, never to return. Eventually, a legal battle ended with him agreeing to let the studio use his recordings mimed by the new star of the film, Edmund Purdom.

Hounded for back taxes and almost pushed to bankruptcy by bad investments made by a former manager, Lanza started to drink heavily and eat greedily. With his weight ballooning, he took his family to his ancestral home of Italy to try to revive his career. It initially seemed to be an inspired move: he cut down on his drinking and started to get his weight under control, and he was fêted throughout Europe. However,

Mario Lanza lost his temper and
a battle with the bottle.

his sudden death from a heart attack in Rome in 1959 triggered
rumours that he was bumped off by the Mafia for refusing to co-operate
with them while in the United States. Five months later, his broken-
hearted widow died of a drug overdose.

But Mario Lanza lives on through recordings that continue to be
in demand (he was the very first artist to have his back catalogue
transferred on to CD). Maria 'The Voice' Callas paid him the ultimate
tribute when she said: 'My biggest regret is not to have had the opportunity to sing with the greatest tenor voice I've ever heard.'

Princess Margaret Few royals – apart from her uncle Edward
(VIII) – could put it away like Princess Margaret, the Queen's
younger sister. She turned to drinking, smoking and having fun
after being prevented by the Establishment from marrying her one
true love, Group-Captain Peter Townsend, who was a divorcé at
a time when that was a big deal for the royal family.

It was a well-known fact that she chain-smoked up to sixty

Chesterfields a day, and she drank Famous Grouse whisky heavily at home. During her headline-hitting holidays on the sub-tropical island paradise of Mustique she switched to gin, and was rumoured to have had a series of flings that kept MI5 on their toes keeping the scandals out of the tabloids.

Among her conquests were said to have been Peter Sellers, Robin Douglas-Home, Roddy Llewellyn, and tough-guy Cockney gangster turned actor John Bindon, whose favourite party trick was balancing five half-pints of beer on his manhood!

There was also talk of Bindon having 'By Royal Appointment' tattooed on his most prized possession, but Margaret said if he did she'd crown him. (OK, I made that last bit up.)

Joe McCarthy This 'son-of-a-bitch' Senator (as he was known to his political rivals) wrecked hundreds of lives with his mostly unfounded accusations against 'communist sympathisers' during his witch-hunt in the 1950s. This was when the Cold War with the Soviet Union was at its most dangerous, and anyone with left-wing leanings was considered close to the Devil.

McCarthy made scatter-gun accusations against dozens of public figures, particularly in Hollywood, and had them blacklisted as potential Soviet spies. 'Are you or have you ever been a member of the Communist Party?' became a chilling question asked over and over again in televised trials of prominent American citizens. Although many were let off the ordeal of a trial for 'naming names' of others.

After four years of wild allegations, fair-minded Senators at last had the guts to stand up to McCarthy as they realised that most of his claims were unfounded. He was eventually censured and totally discredited.

Only after he had been silenced did it emerge that throughout his reign of terror he had been hiding his own dark secret: he was a chronic alcoholic. He died in 1957 of cirrhosis of the liver aged just forty-eight, but in his short life he had managed to turn America into a paranoid nation that was constantly looking for 'reds under the beds'.

Eugene O'Neill America's award-winning playwright managed the fairly unique double of being born in and dying in a hotel bedroom. The son of an Irish actor, O'Neill was born on Broadway in a hotel where his parents were staying during the run of a play. He died sixty-five years later in a Boston hotel where he had spent his last years battling alcoholism.

Between this entrance and exit he gained a reputation as one of the finest dramatists of his time, with nearly all of his plays steeped in a depression that marked his life. He had one son who was an alcoholic, another addicted to heroin, and he disowned his eighteen-year-old daughter Oona when she ran off with fifty-four-year-old movie legend Charlie Chaplin.

But throughout it all he managed to keep writing brilliantly: he was awarded the prestigious Nobel Prize for Literature in 1936, and also won four Pulitzer Prizes, the last one posthumously for *Long Day's Journey into Night*. In that play his main characters drink heavily throughout. It was not performed until 1956, three years after his death, but when it was it was instantly hailed as his masterpiece. He had written it back in 1941 and presented the manuscript to his third wife Carlotta on their twelfth wedding anniversary that year, with a dedication that read:

Dearest: I give you the original script of this play of old sorrow, written in tears and blood. A sadly inappropriate gift, it would seem, for a day celebrating happiness. But you will understand. I mean it as a tribute to your love and tenderness which gave me the faith in love that enabled me to face my dread at last and write this play – write it with deep pity and understanding and forgiveness for all the four haunted Tyrones. These twelve years, Beloved One, have been a Journey into Light – into love. You know my gratitude. And my love! Gene

It was amazing that O'Neill managed to get even a sentence down on paper. He was often found wandering around train stations not knowing where he was supposed to be going or where he had been.

And, to complete the full house of addictions in his family, Carlotta became hooked on potassium bromide and the marriage floundered, although the couple never divorced.

Despite the depressing themes of his plays, O'Neill was not without his humour. He once found himself – drunk, of course – in a nightclub for the one and only time in his life. They turned the spotlight on him and announced that 'America's greatest living playwright is in the house tonight.' O'Neill stood and bowed.

As he was leaving, he was presented with a bill for sixty dollars. He borrowed the waiter's pencil and scrawled on the bill: 'One bow – sixty dollars.'

Ozzy Osbourne Ozzy featured heavily in an earlier chapter, but he makes an appearance here, too, because his recovery shows how important it is for an alcoholic to have somebody who cares to help pull them back from the brink. In Ozzy's case it was his wife Sharon.

She watched with increasing horror as her husband indulged in behaviour that was, as she has described it, 'bizarre, bewildering, grossly offensive and, ultimately, dangerously violent'. Sharon could just about handle his drunken disappearances and his attempts to bring groupies back to their hotel room, but when he tried to strangle her while drunk out of his head she realised that he desperately needed help.

It was then that she put the wheels in motion for a series of recovery programmes. He fell off the wagon countless times, but Sharon persevered and helped nurse Ozzy back to the sober world, and since then he has become an even bigger idol than when he was a drunken rock legend with Black Sabbath.

In short, Ozzy owes Sharon his life. Infamous for his machine-gun use of the f-word, he now knows he has to swear off drink.

Matthew Perry At the peak of his popularity in the smash-hit *Friends* sitcom, actor Matthew Perry was fighting both alcohol and drug addiction. Scenes would be hastily rewritten to cover his absences from the set, and he was hospitalised several times under false names. He has been in and out of rehab since 1997.

Perry, who played the show's most witty character, Chandler, thought he had his dependency beaten, but when *Friends* ended he was suddenly back in crisis. 'I got overconfident thinking I had the thing beat,' he admitted. 'I was a year and nine months sober when I just stopped doing the things I needed to do. I had relaxed and kidded myself that everything was under control. Next thing you know, I had a margarita in my hand and I was buying some dope.'

As he started the downward spiral again his former cast-mates made a pact to be there for him on the end of the telephone if ever he needed their support. That's what friends are for.

He was 'concentrating on my sobriety' in 2007 and getting stuck into new television commitments. He could yet be a famous *ex*-drunk.

Kim Philby Now here's a bloke I wish had choked on his drink. Philby was a member of the spy ring known as the Cambridge Five, along with Donald Maclean, Guy Burgess, Anthony Blunt and John Cairncross. Of the five, Philby did the most damage to British and American intelligence, providing classified information to the Soviet Union that caused the deaths of scores of agents.

They had wormed their way so far into the British Establishment that Philby had been awarded an OBE, and Blunt was an art adviser to the

Queen. All the time they were tapping into British government secrets and passing them to their Russian bosses.

Burgess and Maclean defected to Russia in the fifties, just before an MI5 net closed on them. At that time, Philby was questioned but cleared of being the 'Third Man'. He happily went back to his spying for another decade, and finally nipped off to his spiritual home of the Soviet Union in 1963, just as a Russian defector fingered him. It's amazing that he got away with it for so long, because towards the end of his time in Britain there was hardly a day when he was sober.

He was given a hero's welcome in Moscow, where in 1965 he was awarded the Order of the Red Banner, one of the Soviet Union's highest honours. In the same year, Britain finally stripped him of his OBE. Big deal!

But the Soviets had no more use for him once he had been exposed, and he spent his years in exile as a hopeless alcoholic drowning in a sea of vodka.

Maclean also died an alcoholic. I would definitely have slipped something in their drinks.

George Reeves The original Superman, George Reeves starred in 104 episodes on television and became so identified with the role that he struggled to get any other work. Film folklore has it that scenes of him appearing as a sergeant in the classic *From Here to Eternity* were cut because preview audiences kept shouting, 'Is it a bird? Is it a plane? No, it's Superman!' every time he appeared on screen.

George turned to the bottle in his frustration at not being able to find work. In June 1959, after a night's heavy drinking, he was found shot dead in his bedroom. The coroner's verdict was suicide, but rumours have persisted that he was murdered by either a jealous husband or his wife. This theory was a focal point of the 2006 movie *Hollywoodland*, which starred Ben Affleck as George.

Authorities were said to have settled on the suicide verdict rather than upset the millions of kids who hero-worshipped George and would have been devastated to read 'Superman

Murdered' headlines. It's strange that they thought 'Superman Blows His Brains Out' was preferable.

Diana Ross The Supremes singer, who enjoyed even more success when going solo, started to hit the bottle later in her career. After being jailed on a drink-driving charge, she checked into a Californian rehab centre 'to sort out a few personal issues'.

I always wondered if she was drunk during the opening ceremony of the 1994 World Cup finals in Chicago. She had to take a penalty from all of three yards . . . and missed by at least five feet. The goal still collapsed as had been rehearsed even though the ball was nowhere near it.

It was not her Supreme moment.

Ann Robinson There was a time when 'Queen of Mean' Ann Robinson was the weakest link due to too much drink. She has candidly admitted that alcohol had gained such a hold on her that she was just weeks from death. She was struggling to function in her role as a journalist and returned home to Liverpool to rediscover herself.

In 1978 she swore never to drink again, the same year that Jimmy Greaves gave up alcohol.

Her recovery and fightback to become a television celebrity on both sides of the Atlantic is an inspiration for anybody who feels that the bottle is beating them.

Charlie Sheen His success in back-to-back TV comedy hits *Spin City* and *Two and a Half Men* prove that you can turn your life around. Charlie had seemed unemployable after a series of alcohol/drug/sex-related controversies kept him in the headlines for all the wrong reasons.

His most humiliating moment came when he was called to give evidence at the 1995 trial of a Hollywood madam. He confessed in the witness box that he had spent fifty thousand dollars on a total of twenty-seven prostitutes.

But the slide had begun much earlier. Charlie gave a remarkably frank interview about his off-set behaviour during the making of *Wall Street* in the eighties:

> *I'd begun drinking all the time when the film was under way. We shot in New York City, so I'd be out to the bars every night till three or four in the morning, then try to show up for a six o'clock call to stand toe to toe with Michael Douglas and handle 50 per cent of a scene. How could that work? Yet there I was, the guy that struck gold, looking around at dawn to find that the only one still partying was me. I'd be drinking away, doing blow [cocaine], popping pills, and telling myself I wasn't an addict, because there wasn't a needle stuck in my arm. Talk about mixing up fantasy and reality! My true addiction was alcohol. The extra toxic boosters just helped me shore up the wall between my celebrity self and my real self. The questions I was running from were: 'Is this success all a fluke? Had I been fooling everybody so far? Will I get caught?' It was easy to get hammered and messed up. But in doing so, I buried my self-respect, I buried my self-esteem, I buried my creative drive, and I damned near buried myself.*

Somehow he managed to get clean by 2000 to emerge as one of America's favourite TV sitcom actors.

Joseph Stalin Put any two of the other drunks in this list up against Joseph Stalin in a drinking contest and he would have drunk them both under the table. Perhaps he had the little matter of the deaths of twenty-five million of his countrymen on his conscience? Whatever the reason, he drank enough vodka in his lifetime to have launched the Russian fleet.

Russian dictator Joseph Stalin saw red as the biggest boozer of them all.

It is reliably reported that when Hitler ordered the sneak attack on Russia in 1941, it took Stalin eight days to respond because he was in the middle of a bender. His exploits make one of his drink-sodden successors, Boris Yeltsin, seem sober by comparison.

What this means is that while the Second World War was raging, two of the three leaders of the Allies – Stalin and Churchill – were often blotto!

And both Stalin and Hitler were clinically mad! In 1927 three psychiatrists diagnosed the Russian leader as suffering from para-noia. They were quickly proved 100 per cent correct when, within three days, each of them was murdered as the mad dictator started a purge of thousands of intellectuals.

The son of a drunkard who used to beat him unmercifully, young revolutionary Joseph decided on a change of name because he wanted to preserve no memory of his father. He picked Stalin, meaning 'man of steel', in place of his original name Vissarionio-vich Dzhugashvili (try saying that after a few vodkas).

His paranoia, and his huge capacity for vodka, continued to his dying day. He died suddenly on 5 March 1953 in somewhat mysterious circumstances, after announcing his intention to arrest Jewish doctors in the Kremlin, whom he believed were plotting to kill him.

Although affectionately known as 'Uncle Joe' during the Second World War, he will be remembered as the biggest mass killer of them all. And he ordered many of them while in an alcoholic haze.

Cheerski my arse!

Dylan Thomas The Welsh poet seemed almost proud to have become a legless legend in his own lifetime. He used to boast about his capacity for drink, and believed he produced his best work when warmed by whisky.

To go with his extraordinary writing talent he had a beautifully pitched speaking voice almost on a par with that of his great friend Richard Burton, who gave the finest rendition of Thomas's *Under Milk Wood*. The author himself made more than two hundred broadcasts for the BBC, mainly on the highbrow Third Programme. When reading his poems he was often heavily under the influence of either his favourite Beefeater Gin or his 'second favourite but mightily dangerous' whisky. While others were eating, he would hug a glass of Scotch and say: 'Fine nosh, this.'

Everything about his short life was like something out of a novelist's imagination. He saw Irish dancer Caitlin MacNamara through an alcoholic fog as she sat at a bar in a London pub in 1936. Having pushed his way through the throng of drinkers, he put his head in her lap and proposed marriage. She accepted and they were still married at the time of his death in November 1953 while on a poetry-reading tour of the United States. Shortly before the end, in New York, he boasted of having drunk eighteen straight whiskies, claiming it as a record. His last words as he lay dying of pneumonia were: 'After thirty-nine years, this is all I've done.'

But his name will always live on as the Bard of Wales.

Dick Van Dyke Yes, it's true! The star of *Diagnosis Murder, The Dick Van Dyke Show* and most famously the cheeky chimney-sweep in *Mary Poppins* had many lost years in the 1970s when he was secretly filling himself with booze. The world of show-business was shocked when he announced that he was an alcoholic, but he finally overcame his dependency after turning to Alcoholics Anonymous and rehab. In a television 'confession' he admitted:

> *I thought I would come out, because there was such a strange perception about alcoholism. There was this widely held belief that people had serious character flaws. They had weak wills or something. They had this image of, you know, a guy laying in the street and on skid row, whereas it can happen to normal, average middle-class guys, or perfectly respectable ladies. I was never drunk in public. I did my drinking in private, one Martini leading to two and so on. I really believe there is a gene. Some people become addicted and others don't. There should be no stigma attached to it.*

Dick, who has always considered himself more a song-and-dance man than an actor, had been dry for more than twenty years coming into 2007 and approaching, unbelievably, his eighty-fifth birthday.

I just wonder if he was sozzled when he learned how to talk 'Cockney' for *Mary Poppins*. Cor blimey, if that was Cock-er-ney, mate, then I'm a bleedin' Dutchman.

Orson Welles How sad that a man who was once the young uncrowned King of Hollywood should finish up as a laughing stock. One of the most watched video clips on *YouTube* shows Welles, obviously drunk, slurring his words as he makes a total mess of a commercial for an American wine. Millions of youngsters have giggled at this sad sight and take it as representative of Orson Welles, who comes across as a pissed old fart. But the commercial was shot in the days when his main meal every day consisted of two steaks and a pint of whisky. Earlier in life he had been a pioneering giant of the film industry, a creative director and producer, and the star of such classics as *The Third Man*, *The Stranger*, *The Trial* and *The Lady from Shanghai*.

He turned to the bottle when he became almost a caricature of himself, and relied on commercials to pay the rent. He was also a glutton, once eating eighteen hotdogs in one sitting at an LA restaurant. His weight eventually ballooned to twenty-five stone.

But even as he gasped for breath in his later years he remained as witty and sharp as ever . . .

'Donny Osmond has the ear for music of Van Gogh.'

'I started at the top and worked my way down.'

'I hate television as much as I hate peanuts, and I can't stop eating peanuts.'

'A film studio is the biggest train set a boy ever had.'

'My doctor has ordered me to stop having intimate dinners for four, unless there are three other people at the table with me.'

I prefer to think of him as the young genius who made *Citizen Kane* – one of the all-time great films – rather than the old drunk being mocked on the internet.

Amy Winehouse In her short career, this sharp-tongued Cockney singer/songwriter has already gathered a huge following with performances that come right from the soul. She makes no secret of her appetite for drink, and is constantly in the tabloid and music press as a result of her drunken escapades. She truly seems to be trying to live up to her name.

She has appeared drunk on television at least twice, on the *Charlotte Church Show* and *Never Mind the Buzzcocks*, and boozily heckled U2 lead singer Bono during an awards show acceptance speech. She lets the f-word drop like a navvy, and has often been involved in unladylike drunken brawls.

Asked about her actions when drunk, she once admitted: 'I have a really good time some nights, but then I push it over the edge and ruin my boyfriend's night. I'm an ugly dickhead drunk, I really am.'

Well, she said it.

Amy has since married her boyfriend, Blake Fielder-Civil. I hope all their troubles are small (and sober) ones.

Gig Young There is a widely held superstition in Hollywood that winning an Oscar can prove a curse. Gig Young is one of the actors held up as proof that there is truth in the tale.

He won his Academy Award for a captivating performance as the MC in the harrowing 1969 dance film *They Shoot Horses, Don't They?* From there on it was downhill all the way for Gig, ending in a double tragedy too gruesome for even a Hollywood scriptwriter to have created.

In the early seventies, he became a desperate drunk, admitting in an interview: 'Since winning the Oscar, nothing has gone right for me. Like so many before me, I've had nothing but bad luck.' He felt the award had been the kiss of death.

It all came to a terrible climax when he suffered a nightmare attack of the DTs on the first day of filming *Blazing Saddles* in 1974. Director Mel Brooks replaced him with Gene Wilder, who got huge laughs by *faking* the same condition in the finished movie.

Just three weeks after marrying his fifth wife (she was thirty-one, he was sixty-four) the couple were found shot dead in their New York City apartment. The inquest found that Young had shot his wife and then himself in a suicide pact.

Lying alongside their bodies was the Oscar statuette.

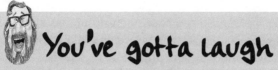

You've gotta laugh

The French colonel was new to his post as commander of a Foreign Legion fort in the middle of the desert. He has been weeks without the company of a woman, so one night in the officers' mess he quietly asks his adjutant: 'Tell me, Jacques, what do the men do for their, uh, you know, pleasure?'

Jacques confides: 'We takes turns to use Brigitte.'

The colonel cannot believe his ears. Brigitte was the almost clapped-out camel that had been adopted as the fort's mascot. '*All* the men use her?' he asks.

Jacques shrugs. 'What else are we to do here in the middle of nowhere with the nearest town ten kilometres away?'

The colonel cannot face the prospect, and forces it out of his mind. But one night three weeks later, with his defences weakened by too much drink, he gives in to his frustration and quietly leads Brigitte into a dark, deserted corner of the parade ground.

After an hour of huffing and puffing and struggling to keep the camel still, he finally has his way.

The colonel is sitting in an exhausted, drunken heap alongside the equally exhausted Brigitte when Jacques walks up with his arms spread wide. 'What on earth have you done, Colonel?' he asks.

'What do you think I've done?' the colonel replies, bemused by the shocked look on his adjutant's face.

'Each to his own,' says Jacques, 'but we use Brigitte to ride into town to visit the local brothel.'

Hark Who's Talking About Drink

'I drink too much. The last time I gave a urine sample it had an olive in it.'
– Rodney Dangerfield

'I always know when I've had enough to drink, but the realisation always comes a drink or three too late.'
– Charles Hawtrey

'Better to be occasionally drunk than permanently sober.'
– Orson Welles

'The more I think, the more I drink, and now I'm drunk I thunk.'
– John Edwards

'Drinking is a good way of ending the day, and it can also give it a good start.'
– Ernest Hemingway

'I'd rather the company of a drunken clown than a sober judge.'
– Michael Bentine

'Trying to entertain a drunken audience is like trying to be funny on the deck of the *Titanic*.'
– Bob Monkhouse

'The only thing I liked about *The Lost Weekend* [a film about an alcoholic] was the drinking.'
– Dorothy Parker

'Women need a reason to drink; men just need a drink.'
– Billy Crystal

'I have been drunk and I have been sober. Weighing the two conditions up carefully and after thorough analysis I have come to the conclusion that on the whole I prefer being drunk.'
– Graham Chapman

'I follow the doctor's orders to have only one glass of wine a night. I then drink the rest direct from the bottle.'
– Tommy Cooper

11 A Man Walks into a Bar

Last orders! Having been brought up on the northern club circuit, I know the importance of the old saying: 'Always leave 'em laughing.' So for my final chapter I have collected the funniest pub jokes that start with the time-honoured words 'A man walks into a bar . . .' Thanks for your company and letting me have my shout. Now get your laughing gear around this cocktail of classics and more corn than you will find in a chiropodist's surgery . . .

A man walks into a bar . . . drawn by the sound of a rocking piano. He looks in the direction of the piano in the corner and wonders why he can't see the pianist.

On closer inspection he discovers a tiny man, just a foot tall, standing on the keyboard and playing away.

'I've never seen a pianist quite like him,' he says to the landlord, while ordering a drink. 'Where did he come from?'

'It's a long story and I haven't got time to tell it,' the landlord says. 'Here, rub this and you will find out quick enough how I got him.'

He hands the man a lamp, and as he rubs it a genie suddenly appears.

'What is your wish, Master?' asks the bowing genie.

'Uh, can you manage a million pounds?' the man asks, not truly believing what he is seeing.

'Your wish is granted, Master,' says the genie, clapping his hands and then disappearing back into the lamp.

Just as the man thinks his wish has been ignored a million dogs come racing through the bar.

Realising what has gone wrong, the man yells into the lamp, 'Hey, I didn't ask for a million hounds.'

The landlord shrugs and says: 'You don't think I asked for a twelve-inch *pianist*, either, do you?'

A man walks into a bar . . . and round his neck he has two car jump leads.

The landlord says: 'You can come in, sir, but don't start anything!'

A man walks into a bar . . . and says to the barman, 'Give me a beer before there's big trouble!'

The barman feels intimidated and pulls a pint.

After sinking the drink in one go, the man roars: 'Give me another beer before there's big trouble!'

Again the timid barman pulls a pint. The man sinks it in one go and then demands: 'Give me another beer before there's big trouble.'

After five pints have disappeared down the man's throat the barman finally gets the confidence to ask: 'When are you going to pay for these beers?'

'Ah,' says the man, 'now there's going to be big trouble.'

A man walks into a bar . . . accompanied by an emu. The barman asks what they want. The man says: 'A gin and tonic for me and a packet of cheese and onion crisps.' He turns to the emu: 'What's yours?'

'I'll have the same,' says the emu.

The barman serves them and says: 'That will be six pounds seventy-five pence, please.'

The man reaches into his pocket and pulls out the exact money.

Next day, the man and the emu come into the same bar. 'A large vodka and tonic and a mushroom omelette from the kitchen,' he says.

'Same for me,' says the emu.

'That will be nineteen pounds forty-five pence,' the barman says.

Again the man takes the exact money from his pocket.

For the next six nights the man and the emu order identical drinks and snacks, and every time the man reaches into his pocket he pulls out the right money.

The barman can't hold back his curiosity any longer. 'Hope you don't mind my asking, sir,' he says, 'but how come you always manage to find the exact change?'

'Well,' the man explains, 'a few months ago I was cleaning the attic and found an old lamp. When I rubbed it a genie appeared and offered me two wishes. My first wish was that if I ever had to pay for anything, I would just put my hand in my pocket and the right amount of money would always be there.'

'That was a great wish,' says the barman. 'Most people would wish for a million pounds or something, but you'll be rich for as long as you live!'

'That's right,' says the man. 'Whether it's a pint of milk or a Rolls-Royce, the exact money is always there.'

'You're so right,' the emu says.

The barman cannot resist asking one more question. 'Excuse me prying, sir, but what's with the emu?'

The man sighs, looks towards the emu and explains: 'My second wish was for a tall bird with long legs who agrees with everything I say.'

A man goes into a bar . . . with a giraffe at his side. They have been on a pub crawl and after a couple more drinks the giraffe passes out and falls over. The man opens the pub door, about to stagger out by himself, when the barman shouts: "Oi! You can't leave that lyin' there!'

The man turns around and slurs: 'Don't be stupid. He's not a lion. He's a giraffe!'

A man walks into a bar . . . and under his arm he has a slab of tarmac. 'A beer please,' he says, 'and one for the road.'

A man walks into a bar . . . and sits down next to an old lady who has a dog curled up at her feet. The man asks: 'Does your dog bite?'

The lady answers: 'Never.'

The man reaches out to pet the dog, which reacts by biting his hand.

'I thought you said your dog doesn't bite!' he says angrily.

'That isn't my dog,' the old lady replies.

A man walks into a bar . . . and is amazed to find a horse behind the bar serving drinks.

He stands there staring at the horse, his mouth gaping.

'What are you staring at?' the horse asks. 'Haven't you ever seen a horse serving drinks before?'

The man says: 'It's not that. I just never thought the parrot would sell the place.'

A man walks into a bar . . . with a dog on a lead. The barman says, 'Hey, fella, can't you read that sign? It says, "No Dogs Allowed"! Get that mutt out of here!'

The man replies: 'No, I can't read the sign – I'm blind, and this is my guide dog.'

Embarrassed, the barman apologises and gives the man a beer on the house.

Later that day, the man tells his friend how he had managed to con the barman: 'I told him that I was blind and I got a free beer!'

Determined to pull off the same scam, his friend takes his dog into the bar and sits down.

The barman says, 'Oi, can't you read? The sign says, "No Dogs Allowed"! You'll have to leave.'

The friend uses the tried and tested script: 'Sorry, I can't see the sign because I'm blind, and this is my guide dog.'

Suspicious, the barman replies, 'Oh yeah? Since when do they give out poodles as guide dogs?'

The man reaches down, pats the dog and says: 'What? They gave me a *poodle*?'

A man walks into a bar . . . and under his arm he is holding an alligator. He asks the barman: 'Do you serve traffic wardens here?'

'Of course we do,' says the barman.

'Good,' says the man. 'Give me a whisky, and I'll have a traffic warden for my alligator.'

A man walks into a bar . . . with a newt on his shoulder.

'That's an interesting companion you've got there,' the barman says. 'What's his name?'

'Tiny,' the man replies.

'Why do you call him that?' the bartender asks.

'Because he's my newt.'

A man walks into a bar . . . on his own and orders two pints. He does this for ten successive nights. Always on his own, always two pints.

The barman eventually has to ask, 'Sir, excuse me, but why do you always ask for two drinks rather than one at a time?'

'I used to come here with my best friend,' the man replies. 'Sadly he recently died, and I'm drinking the second beer on his behalf.'

A few days later, the man orders just one pint.

'Why only one beer tonight, sir?' asks the barman.

The man explains: 'I've given up drinking!'

A man walks into a bar . . . and finds a stranger behind the bar. 'I'll have a pint of bitter, please,' he says.

The bloke behind the bar pulls him a pint. 'That'll be one penny, please.'

'A penny? Wow!'

The man pays up, and asks to see the menu. 'I'll have a fillet steak, medium,' he says. 'French fries, peas and a tomato salad.'

'Certainly, sir,' says his host. 'That'll be threepence.'

'Threepence?' the customer says. 'That's crazy. Where's the usual landlord?'

'Oh, he's upstairs with my wife.'

'What's he doing with your wife?' the customer asks.

'Exactly the same as I'm doing with his business.'

A man walks into a bar ... and the landlord says pleasantly: 'Good evening, sir, what'll you have?'

The man answers, 'A large whisky, please.'

The landlord hands him the drink, and says: 'That'll be four pounds.'

'You must be joking,' the man says. 'I don't owe you a penny. You asked me what I wanted, and I gratefully accepted a drink from you.'

The landlord's mouth was making goldfish movements. 'You don't think you're going to get away with that do you, pal?' he manages to say.

A lawyer sitting nearby has heard the whole conversation. 'You know, he's got you there,' he says to the landlord. 'In the original offer, which constitutes a binding contract upon acceptance, there was no stipulation of remuneration.'

The landlord is fuming, but knows that he has to accept what the lawyer says. 'OK,' he barks to the customer. 'You got a free drink out of me. But don't ever let me catch you in here again.'

The next day, the man walks nonchalantly back into the bar. 'What the heck are you doing back in here?' the landlord says, turning purple. 'I can't believe you've got the nerve to come back.'

The man says: 'What are you talking about? I've never been in this place in my life.'

The landlord looks at him closely and thinks he must have made a mistake. 'I'm very sorry,' he says. 'It's uncanny. You must have a double.'

'Thanks very much,' the man says. 'Make it a whisky.'

A man walks into a bar ... and summons the landlord. 'Tell me, squire, are you a gambling man?' he asks.

The landlord says: 'I love a bet. What have you got in mind?'

'I'll bet you fifty pounds that I can lick my right eye.'

The landlord considers this and then agrees to the bet.

The man puts a hand to his face, pulls out his glass right eye and licks it.

With a groan, the landlord grudgingly hands over fifty quid and tells the man to leave his pub.

A week later, the same man walks into the bar. He goes up to the landlord and asks: 'Are you still a betting man, squire?'

Not wanting to lose face, the landlord replies: 'I'll always be a betting man, but you won't catch me out this time.'

'OK, squire,' the man says. 'This time I'll bet you one hundred pounds that I can bite my left eye.'

The landlord recalls that he had a glass right eye, so he couldn't possibly have a removable left one as well. 'Go on then,' he says after careful consideration. 'You've got a bet.'

The man puts a hand to his mouth, pulls out his dentures and clicks them on his left eye. Annoyed with himself, the landlord pays up and again tells the man to get out of his pub.

The following week, the same man ventures into the pub and yet again approaches the landlord. 'Still a betting man, squire?' he asks.

As the pub is packed, the landlord does not want to back down in front of so many witnesses. 'You know what I've told you before. I'll *always* be a betting man. But don't think you can catch me out three times in a row.'

'OK, squire,' says the man. 'For one hundred notes I bet if I spin round on this stool you can't stop me long enough to pull down my trousers and kiss my arse. You have just one minute to do it, otherwise I win.'

The landlord is a former weightlifter who still prides himself on his strength. 'You're on,' he says. 'I'll take that bet.'

As he comes round from the other side of the bar, the man starts to spin around on the stool. The landlord quickly reaches out, stops him spinning and gets him in a half nelson. Then he flips him over, pulls down his trousers and triumphantly plants a quick peck on his arse.

'Well done, squire,' the man says sportingly. 'That was brilliant. Here's your hundred notes.'

He hands back the hundred quid the landlord had given him the previous week, and warmly shakes his hand.

'I have to admit you're a good loser,' the landlord says, giving him a free Scotch.

'Oh, I haven't lost, squire,' the man says. 'I bet thirty of the people in this bar fifty quid each that you would kiss my arse within five minutes of me sitting on that stool.'

YES, CHEERS MY ARSE!